INDIVIDUALISED M

Developed by the School Math
association with the National I

FURTHER ALGEBRA AND COMPUTATION

CAMBRIDGE UNIVERSITY PRESS

Cambridge
London New York New Rochelle
Melbourne Syndey

Published by the Press Syndicate of the University of Cambridge
The Pitt Building, Trumpington Street, Cambridge CB2 1RP
32 East 57th Street, New York, NY 10022, USA
296 Beaconsfield Parade, Middle Park, Melbourne 3206, Australia

First published 1983

Printed in Great Britain at the University Press, Cambridge

Library of Congress catalogue card number: 82-14780

British Library cataloguing in publication data
Individualised mathematics.
Further algebra and computation
1. Mathematics-1961-
I. School Mathematics Project
II. National Extension College
510 QA39.2

ISBN 0 521 27265 3

The School Mathematics Project

When the SMP was founded in 1961, its main objective was to devise radically new secondary school mathematics courses to reflect, more adequately than did the traditional syllabuses, the up-to-date nature and usages of mathematics. The first texts produced embodied new courses for O-level (*SMP Books 1–5*) and A-level (*SMP Advanced Mathematics Books 1–4*). *Books 3, 4* and *5* have now been revised to become *SMP New Book 3, Parts 1* and *2, New Book 4, Parts 1* and *2*, and *New Book 5*, while *Revised Advanced Mathematics Books 1, 2* and *3* cover the syllabus for the A-level examination in SMP Mathematics. Five shorter texts cover the material of the various sections of the A-level examination SMP Further Mathematics. There are two books for SMP Additional Mathematics at O-level. All the SMP GCE examinations are available to schools through any of the GCE examining boards.

Books A–H cover broadly the same development of mathematics as the first few books of the O-level series. Most CSE boards offer appropriate examinations. In practice this series is being used very widely across all streams of comprehensive schools and its first seven books, together with *Books X, Y* and *Z*, provide a course leading to the SMP O-level examination. *SMP Cards I* and *II* provide an alternative treatment in card form of the mathematics in *Books A–D*. The six Units of *SMP 7–13*, designed for children in that age-range, provide a course for middle schools which is also widely used in primary schools and the first two years of secondary schools. Teacher's Guides accompany all these series.

The SMP has produced many other texts and teachers are encouraged to obtain each year from Cambridge University Press, The Edinburgh Building, Shaftesbury Road, Cambridge CB2 2RU, the full list of SMP publications currently available. In the same way, help and advice may always be sought by teachers from the Executive Director at the SMP Office, Westfield College, Kidderpore Avenue, London NW3 7ST.

The Annual Reports, details of forthcoming in-service training courses, SMP syllabuses and other information may be obtained from the same address.

The SMP is continually evaluating old work and preparing for new. The effectiveness of the SMP's work depends, as it has always done, on the comments and reactions received from a wide variety of teachers – and also from pupils – using SMP materials. Readers of the texts can, therefore, send their comments to the SMP in the knowledge that they will be valued and carefully studied.

The authors of the original books on whose work this series is based are named in *The School Mathematics Project: The First Ten Years*, published by the Cambridge University Press.

SMP Individualised Mathematics has been produced by a team consisting of

Judy Bonsall	G. Merlane
G. S. Howlett	L. Savins
M. K. Leach	D. R. Skinner
J. L. Lloyd	J. V. Tyson

John Lloyd led the work on the series until his death in 1977, and the final editing has been carried out by Derek Skinner. Many others have helped with advice and criticism, particularly those students who worked through the material in draft form.

Contents

Preface

SMP Individualised Mathematics is based upon the content of *SMP Books 1–5* and *Books A–G, X, Y, Z*, covering the syllabus for the O-level SMP Mathematics. There are two main distinguishing features of the series. First, the material is presented in a programmed form and the books are thus suitable for use in individualised learning, where self-assessment and clear explanation play a major role. The carefully structured development of each topic makes the books suitable for use by students working alone with minimum tuition, in schools, technical colleges, colleges of further education and on courses organised by the National Extension College.

Secondly, instead of the spiral development of the SMP texts, *SMP Individualised Mathematics* presents the mathematics by topics. Each book, apart from the two devoted to revision, presents the work on a particular theme. Hence the books will prove useful to pupils who have missed work through absence from class, to students coming from abroad, and to pupils transferring to a different school. The style and arrangement of these books should make them very suitable for use by pupils in the sixth form who are working to improve their earlier performance at CSE or O-level. The books will also be useful for revision and consolidation.

Although written with the SMP O-level course in mind, *SMP Individualised Mathematics*, like other SMP texts, can be used to prepare for other O-level examinations based on similar syllabuses.

The titles in this series are as follows:
Computation and Graphs
Probability and Statistics
Algebra 1: Language and Structure
Algebra 2: Equations, Formulas and Graphs
Further Algebra and Computation
Matrix Algebra and Isometric Transformations
Further Matrices and Transformations
Geometry 1: Symmetry and Trigonometry
Geometry 2: Shapes and Similarity
Geometry 3: Three Dimensions
Revision 1
Revision 2

How to use this book

Each chapter begins with a list of what you should be able to do after studying the chapter. This is followed by a pre-test, which gives you some idea of what you should know before you start that particular chapter. If you have difficulty with the pre-test you should revise the work required for it – from either the appropriate chapter of this or a companion book, or an elementary text-book – before continuing with the chapter.

The teaching part of the chapter is divided into several numbered sections, and includes a number of exercises. Other questions are asked in the text, and *you should write down the answers to all these questions and exercises in a notebook* as you go along. The start of each set of questions is marked by a white triangle on the left-hand side of the page. When you come to a triangle with a number in it (on the *right-hand* side of the page) you should check your work to that point by turning to the answers at the end of the chapter and finding the triangle with the same number (now on the *left-hand* side of the page).

The teaching part of the chapter is followed by a summary of the important results of the chapter (you may well find it helpful to copy these into a separate notebook that is kept especially for revision), and a post-test to test your understanding of the chapter as a whole. The answers to this post-test are also at the end of the chapter.

Finally (apart from the answers) there is an 'assignment'. This is another exercise covering the whole chapter, but this time there are no answers in this book. If at all possible you should have *this* exercise marked by a teacher or tutor.

1 Quadratic expressions

Objectives

This is what you should be able to do after studying this chapter.

(1) Recognise a quadratic expression, a quadratic function, and a quadratic equation.
(2) Expand expressions of the form $a(b + c)$ and $(p + q)(r + s)$.
(3) Factorise expressions of the form $ab + ac$ and $x^2 + px + q$.
(4) Sketch and draw the graphs of quadratic functions, and use them to solve quadratic equations.
(5) Know that if M and N are any two numbers or expressions,

$$M \times N = 0 \Leftrightarrow M = 0 \text{ or } N = 0,$$

and use this result to solve certain quadratic equations by factorisation.

Pre-test

1 Simplify the following.
(a) $3(2x + 5)$ (b) $(2 + x)y$ (c) $3(1 - 2x)$
(d) $4x(2 - 3y)$ (e) $1 - 3(x + 2y)$ (f) $5(x + y) - 3(2x + 5y)$

2 $Q = ax^2 + bx + c$.
(a) Write down the expression for Q when $a = 2$, $b = {}^-3$ and $c = 4$.
(b) Evaluate (i.e. work out the value of) Q when $x = 2$.
(c) Evaluate Q when $x = {}^-2$.
(d) Repeat parts (a), (b) and (c) for $a = 1$, $b = 5$ and $c = {}^-2$.

3 Sketch the graphs of the following functions for ${}^-4 \leqslant x \leqslant 4$.
(a) x^2 (b) $3x^2$ (c) $-x^2$ (d) $-\frac{1}{2}x^2$

4 The function f is defined by $f: x \to x^2 - 2x - 3$.
(a) Find the value of $f(x)$ for each of the following values of x.
${}^-2, {}^-1, 0, \frac{1}{2}, 1, 1\frac{1}{2}, 2, 3, 4, 5$
(b) Draw the graph of $y = x^2 - 2x - 3$ for values of x from ${}^-2$ to ${}^+4$.
(c) For what values of x is the value of $f(x)$ zero?

1

1.1 The distributive law

The multiplication $3 \times 5 = 15$ may be interpreted as stating that a rectangle with dimensions 3 cm and 5 cm has an area of 15 cm^2. This is shown in Figure 1.

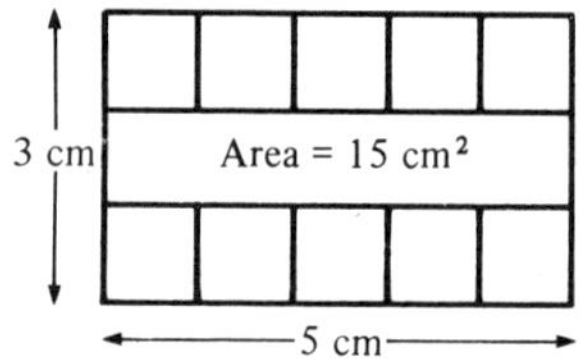

Figure 1

Figure 2 is a similar diagram to show the multiplication 3×27. To make the arithmetic easier, the number 27 is broken up into $20 + 7$.

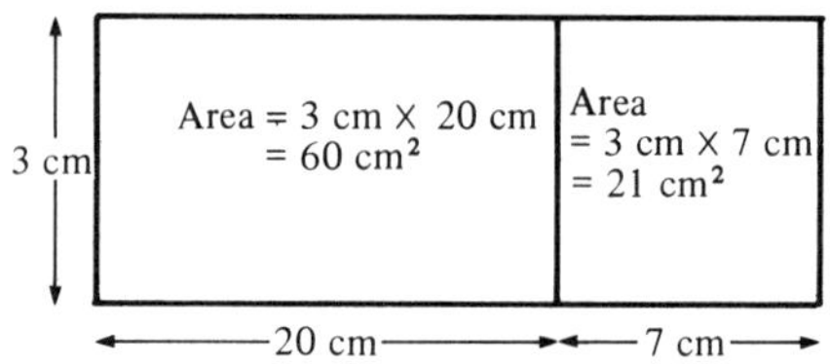

Figure 2

In other words, $3 \times 27 = 3 \times (20 + 7) = 3 \times 20 + 3 \times 7$.
Similarly, $3 \times (x + 7) = 3 \times x + 3 \times 7$,
i.e. $3(x + 7) = 3x + 21$.

In general, $a \times (b + c) = a \times b + a \times c$,
i.e. $a(b + c) = ab + ac$.
As multiplication is commutative, this can also be written as

$$(b + c)a = ba + ca.$$

If a, b and c are real numbers, the last result (in either form) is an identity (i.e. it is true for all values of a, b and c) which illustrates for real numbers the distributive law for multiplication over addition. This means that the 'multiply by a' can be distributed over, or spread over, or combined with, each element in the bracket.

1 Work out the following.
(a) $6 \times 12\frac{1}{2}$ (b) 37×100.2 (c) $3(x + 7)$ (d) $4(3x - 5)$
(e) $6(2x - 3y)$ (f) $x(9 + h)$ (g) $\frac{1}{2}(11 + 6x)$ (h) $(2x + 3y)4z$

2 Work out the following. (Remember that expressions inside brackets are evaluated first.)
(a) $2 + (3 \times 4)$ and $(2 + 3) \times (2 + 4)$
(b) $12 \div (2 + 4)$ and $(12 \div 2) + (12 \div 4)$
(c) $(2 + 4) \div 12$ and $(2 \div 12) + (4 \div 12)$

2

Two brackets

Figure 3(a) shows the multiplication 12×34.

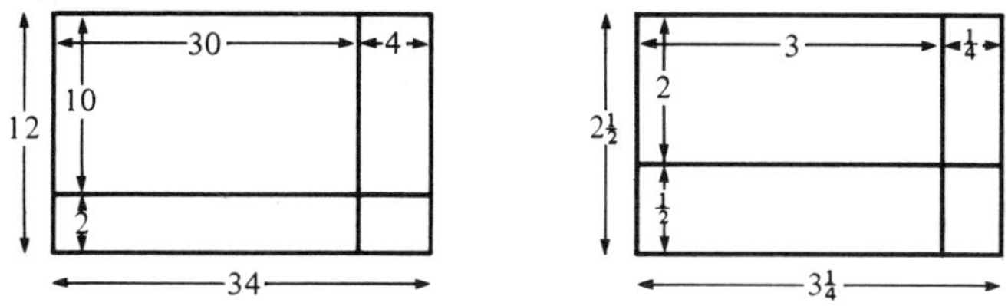

(a) (b) Figure 3

This can be considered as

either $(10 + 2) \times 34$
$= 10 \times 34 + 2 \times 34$
$= 10(30 + 4) + 2(30 + 4)$
$= 10 \times 30 + 10 \times 4 + 2 \times 30 + 2 \times 4$
$= 300 + 40 + 60 + 8.$

or $12 \times (30 + 4)$
$= 12 \times 30 + 12 \times 4$
$= (10 + 2)30 + (10 + 2)4$
$= 10 \times 30 + 2 \times 30 + 10 \times 4 + 2 \times 4$
$= 300 + 60 + 40 + 8.$

The sum is 408 in both cases.

Figure 3(b) shows that $2\frac{1}{2} \times 3\frac{1}{4} = 2 \times 3 + 2 \times \frac{1}{4} + 3 \times \frac{1}{2} + \frac{1}{2} \times \frac{1}{4} = 8\frac{1}{8}$. (Remember that a mixed number such as $2\frac{1}{2}$ means $2 + \frac{1}{2}$. Mixed numbers are therefore the exception to the convention that 'no sign between two numbers means multiply'. Thus $2\frac{1}{2} \times 3\frac{1}{4}$ is **not** equal to $2 \times 3 + \frac{1}{2} \times \frac{1}{4}$.)

Algebraically this may be expressed as

$$(p + q)(r + s) = pr + ps + qr + qs.$$

This expansion is sometimes referred to as 'multiplying out the brackets'; i.e. the expression is rewritten so that there are no brackets on the right-hand side.

Figure 4 shows two possible ways of remembering this result.

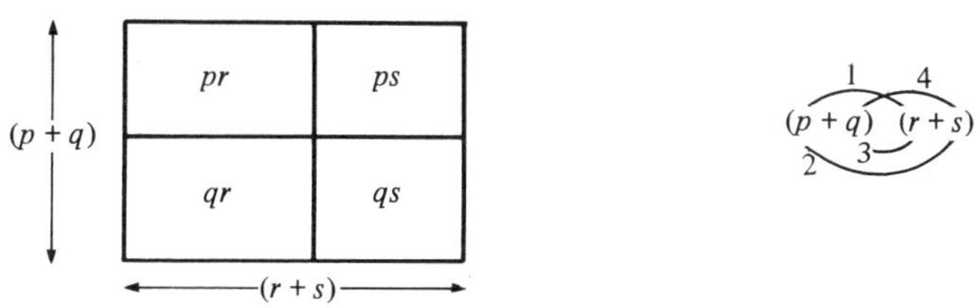

(a) (b) Figure 4

Although it is not so easy to show it diagrammatically, the result is still true when some of the terms p, q, r and s are negative. (The diagrammatic approach is considered in questions 1 and 2 of Exercise A.)

Some examples of this expansion are as follows.

$$51 \times 99 = (50 + 1)(100 - 1) = 5000 - 50 + 100 - 1 = 5049$$
$$(2x + 3)(4y + 5) = 8xy + 10x + 12y + 15$$
$$(2x + 3)(4x + 5) = 8x^2 + 10x + 12x + 15 = 8x^2 + 22x + 15$$
$$(2x + 5)(4x - 3) = 8x^2 - 6x + 20x - 15 = 8x^2 + 14x - 15$$
$$(2 - 3x)(4 - 5x) = 8 - 10x - 12x + 15x^2 = 8 - 22x + 15x^2$$

From the last three examples notice that when both brackets contain a term in the same variable (x in these examples), the two 'middle terms' can often be combined (or 'collected together').

Work out the following, using the methods above.

3 (a) 91×81 (b) 19×41 (c) 101×99

4 (a) $(x+2)(y+5)$ (b) $(x+3)(x+1)$ (c) $(x-3)(x+4)$
(d) $(y+6)(x-5)$ (e) $(x-7)(x-8)$ (f) $(x-2)(y-2)$

5 (a) $(2x+1)(3y+4)$ (b) $(2x+3)(x+5)$ (c) $(3x+4)(5x+6)$
(d) $(2x-1)(3y+4)$ (e) $(2x+3)(x-5)$ (f) $(3x-4)(5x-6)$ 3

6 (a) $(x+4)^2$ [i.e. $(x+4)(x+4)$] (b) $(3x+5)^2$ (c) $(2+9x)^2$
(d) $(x-4)^2$ (e) $(3x-5)^2$ (f) $(2-9x)^2$

7 (a) $(x+7)(x-7)$ (b) $(2x-3)(2x+3)$ (c) $(4+3x)(4-3x)$

8 (a) 51×51 (b) 49×51 (c) 49×49 4

Three useful results

From questions 6, 7 and 8 above we can write down three identities that are worth remembering.

$$\left.\begin{array}{lll} (1) & (a+b)^2 & = a^2+2ab+b^2 \\ (2) & (a-b)^2 & = a^2-2ab+b^2 \\ (3) & (a+b)(a-b) & = a^2-b^2 \end{array}\right\} \text{ for all values of } a \text{ and } b.$$

Exercise A

1 (a) What is the area of the shaded rectangle in Figure 5(a)?
(b) What is the area of the shaded rectangle in Figure 5(b)?

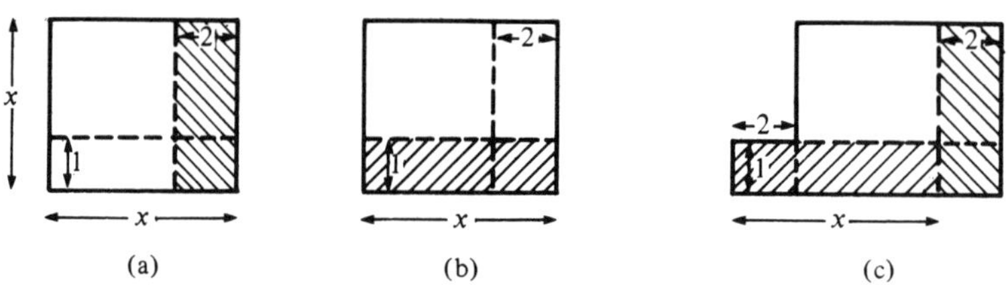

Figure 5

(c) Hence explain how Figure 5(c) may be used to show that

$$(x-2)(x-1) = x^2 - 3x + 2.$$

2 Draw diagrams similar to Figure 5 to show that

$$(x+2)(x-1) = x^2 + x - 2.$$

Work out the following.

3 (a) $(x+2)(x+6)$ (b) $(x-2)(x+6)$
(c) $(x+2)(x-6)$ (d) $(x-2)(x-6)$

4 (a) $(3x+4)(2y+7)$ (b) $(3x-4)(2x+7)$
(c) $(3x+4)(2y-7)$ (d) $(3x-4)(2x-7)$

Write down the expansions of the following.

5 (a) $(x+y)^2$ (b) $(x-y)^2$ (c) $(x+y)(x-y)$ (d) $(x-y)(x+y)$
(e) $(p+q)^2$ (f) $(p-q)^2$ (g) $(q-p)^2$ (h) $(p+q)(q-p)$

6 (a) $(3x+4)^2$ (b) $(3x-4)^2$ (c) $(3x+4)(3x-4)$
(d) $(3x-4)(3x+4)$ (e) $(4-3x)^2$ (f) $(4-3x)(3x+4)$ 5

1.2 Factorisation

If the results of the previous section are reversed, we obtain identities such as

$$
\begin{aligned}
3x + 21 &= 3(x+7) \\
8x^2 + 14x - 15 &= (2x+5)(4x-3) \\
9x^2 - 16 &= (3x+4)(3x-4).
\end{aligned}
$$

When written this way, we say that the expression on the left-hand side has been 'factorised'. For example, 3 and $(x+7)$ are both factors of $3x+21$. (If the value of x is not known, then $(x+7)$ cannot be factorised, and so, algebraically, 3 and $(x+7)$ are the prime factors of $3x+21$.) It is usual, when factorising algebraic expressions, to write the numerical factors as a single number. Thus $36x+48y$ is considered to be 'factorised completely' when written as $12(3x+4y)$; but not when written as $4(9x+12y)$ as the algebraic part $9x+12y$ can be factorised further.

By no means all algebraic expressions are capable of being factorised in the way illustrated at the beginning of this section. The rest of this section considers methods for those expressions for which you expect (or suspect) factorisation to be possible. In most cases it is assumed that the numerical terms or coefficients are whole numbers: the main exception will be in some examples of 'the difference of two squares'.

Expressions with two terms

If an expression containing two terms is capable of being factorised, it is usually of the form

$$ab + ac = a(b+c).$$

In such cases, the factor a is said to be a *common factor*.

1 Factorise the following.
(a) $4y+12$ (b) $3-24y$ (c) $24x+40y$ (d) x^2+3xy
(e) $3xy-12yz$ (f) $10-10z$ (g) z^2-3z 6

The third example at the beginning of this section, $9x^2-16=(3x+4)(3x-4)$, illustrates a special case, which can be generalised as

$$a^2 - b^2 = (a+b)(a-b).$$

This is often referred to as *the difference of two squares*. Some examples of this factorisation are as follows.

$$x^2 - y^2 = (x+y)(x-y) \text{ [or, of course, } (x-y)(x+y)]$$
$$a^2 - 9x^2 = a^2 - (3x)^2 = (a+3x)(a-3x)$$
$$1 - 25z^2 = (1+5z)(1-5z)$$
$$p^2 - 64 = (p+8)(p-8)$$
$$16 - 36y^2 = 4(4-9y^2) = 4((2)^2 - (3y)^2) = 4(2+3y)(2-3y)$$

(Notice that in the last example the common factor was 'taken out' first. Alternatively, the stages of the factorisation could be

$$(4)^2 - (6y)^2 = (4+6y)(4-6y) = 2(2+3y) \times 2(2-3y) = 4(2+3y)(2-3y).)$$

▷ **2** Factorise the following.
(a) $x^2 - q^2$ (b) $x^2 - 4p^2$ (c) $9t^2 - 1$ (d) $36 - u^2$
(e) $16x^2 - 25z^2$ (f) $10m^2 - 40n^2$ (g) $25a^2b - 100bc^2$ 7 ▶

Expressions with three terms

These are a little more difficult to factorise (assuming that factorisation is possible), and to a certain extent the method is one of trial and error; but the 'error' is considerably lessened if you are familiar with evaluating products of the types considered in Section 1.1.

(1) In all factorisations you should first look for any common factors.

(2) Having removed any common factors, it is possible to deduce some methods for expressions of the form $x^2 + px + q$ (where p and q stand for some given numbers), and these are illustrated in the examples below.

▷ **3** Work out the following, and note where pluses and minuses occur in the expansions.
(a) $(x+2)(x+3)$ (b) $(x+2)(x-3)$
(c) $(x-2)(x+3)$ (d) $(x-2)(x-3)$

4 (a) Multiply out $(x+s)(x+t)$.
(b) If the answer to (a) is to be identical to $x^2 + 11x + 24$, write down the values of $(s+t)$ and (st).
(c) Hence find, by trial and error, the values of s and t. 8 ▶

Example 1. Factorise $x^2 + 15x + 36$.

The factors are of the form $(x+s)$ and $(x+t)$, where s and t are both positive, and $s + t = 15$ and $st = 36$.
Possible values that give a product of 36 are

$$(1, 36),\ (2, 18),\ (3, 12),\ (4, 9) \text{ and } (6, 6).$$

The only one of these pairs that gives a sum of 15 is $(3, 12)$.
Hence the factors are $(x+3)$ and $(x+12)$;

i.e. $x^2 + 15x + 36 = (x+3)(x+12)$.

Example 2. Factorise $x^2 - 12x + 36$.

The factors are of the form $(x - s)(x - t)$, such that $s + t = 12$ and $st = 36$. From the pairs listed in Example 1 the one that gives a sum of 12 is $(6, 6)$. Hence $s = 6$ and $t = 6$; and the factorisation is $(x - 6)(x - 6)$.

Example 3. Factorise $x^2 - 16x - 36$.

As the last term (-36) is negative, the factors are of the form $(x + s)(x - t)$ where $st = 36$. In order to give a middle term of -16 the value of t must be greater than that of s, and must be such that $t - s = 16$. From the pairs listed in Example 1, $t = 18$, $s = 2$, and the factors are $(x + 2)(x - 18)$.

Example 4. Factorise $10x^2 + x - 24$, given that one factor is $(2x - 3)$.

Let the other factor be $(px + q)$.
Then $(2x - 3)(px + q) = 10x^2 + x - 24$ (for all values of x).
i.e. $2px^2 \ldots - 3q = 10x^2 \ldots - 24$.
By comparing coefficients (this is permissible, because the factorisation is true for all values of x, and so the two sides of the relation above are identical) $p = 5$ and $q = 8$. (Now check that the 'middle terms' agree by multiplying out $(2x - 3)(5x + 8)$.)
Hence the factorisation is $(2x - 3)(5x + 8)$.

Exercise B

▷ 1 (a) Which of the following is the correct factorisation of $x^2 + 7x + 12$?
$(x + 2)(x + 6)$, $(x + 3)(x + 4)$, $(x + 1)(x + 12)$
(b) Which of the following is the correct factorisation of $x^2 + 10x - 24$?
$(x + 6)(x - 4)$, $(x - 6)(x + 4)$, $(x + 12)(x - 2)$, $(x - 12)(x + 2)$

2 Factorise the following.
(a) $16 + 4b$ (b) $d^2 + 3bcd$ (c) $5g - gh$ (d) $3d + 27d^2$
(e) $2ab + 6bc - 12abc$ (f) $s^2 - 64t^2$ (g) $98k^2 - 50m^2n^2$
(h) $x^2 - 8x + 12$ (i) $x^2 + 6x - 16$ (j) $x^2 - 3x - 40$

3 Use the three identities at the end of Section 1.1 to factorise the following.
(a) $x^2 - 10x + 25$ (b) $4x^2 + 20x + 25$ (c) $x^2 - 169$

4 Find the second factor in each of the following.
(a) $x^2 + 7x - 60 = (x + 12)(\quad)$
(b) $2x^2 - 5x + 2 = (2x - 1)(\quad)$
(c) $3x^2 + 5x - 2 = (x + 2)(\quad)$
(d) $20x^2 - 19x + 3 = (5x - 1)(\quad)$

▶ 9

1.3 Quadratic functions

Functions in one variable (usually x) of the forms

$$f\colon\ x \to ax^2 + bx + c \qquad \text{or} \qquad y = ax^2 + bx + c$$

are known as *quadratic functions*. The right-hand side of such a function, $ax^2 + bx + c$, is called a *quadratic expression*. A quadratic expression contains a *term* in x^2, but no higher power of x. (A quadratic expression contains three terms altogether, ax^2, bx, and c; either or both of the last two may be zero.)

The numbers a, b and c are called the *coefficients*. For example, in the expression $x^2 - 5x + 4$ the coefficient of x^2 is 1, the coefficient of (the term in) x is $^{-}5$, and the constant term/coefficient is $^{+}4$, or simply 4. Notice that this implies that the expression should really be considered as

$$+(1)x^2 + (^{-}5)x + (^{+}4).$$

The graph of a quadratic function is often required. The basic techniques for drawing the graph of a function are described in Chapter 3 of *Computation and Graphs*. The curve so obtained is called a *parabola*. If the curve shown in Figure 6 below is rotated through 180° about the y-axis, a solid shell is formed which is the basis of the parabolic reflectors used in a range of instruments from torches to astronomical telescopes.

The simplest quadratic function, $f\colon x \to x^2$, is shown in Figure 6. The graph of any other quadratic function can be obtained from Figure 6 by a combination of one or more of a translation, a positive stretch, and a reflection in the x-axis.

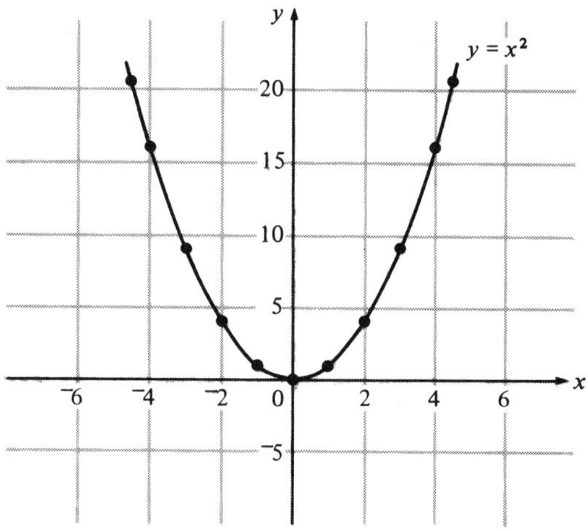

Figure 6

▷ 1 Make an accurate copy of Figure 6, for values of x from $^{-}4\frac{1}{2}$ to $^{+}4\frac{1}{2}$, using scales of 1 cm to 1 unit on the x-axis and 1 cm to 2 units on the y-axis.

2 Complete the following tables, and draw the graphs of these functions on your answer to question 1.

(a) $y = x^2 - 5$

x	$^-5$	$^-4$	$^-2$	0	2	4	5
y	20						

(b) $y = (x + 2)^2$

x	$^-6$	$^-4$	$^-2$	0	2
y	16				

(c) $y = \frac{1}{4}x^2$

x	$^-6$	$^-4$	$^-2$	0	2	4	6
y	9						

(d) $y = 10 - \frac{1}{2}x^2$

x	$^-5$	$^-4$	$^-2$	0	2	4	5
y	$^-2\frac{1}{2}$						

3 Describe a transformation that would map $y = x^2$ onto each part of question 2. **10**

If a quadratic expression can be factorised, the table for the graph of the function can be completed as shown below.

Example 5. $y = x^2 - 5x + 4$
$= (x - 1)(x - 4)$

x	0	1	2	3	4	5
$(x - 1)$	$^-1$	0	1	2	3	4
$(x - 4)$	$^-4$	$^-3$	$^-2$	$^-1$	0	1
y	4	0	$^-2$	$^-2$	0	4

(The values of y are found by multiplying together the corresponding values for $(x - 1)$ and $(x - 4)$.)

▷ **4** (a) Use the table above to draw the graph of $y = x^2 - 5x + 4$. (You will find it useful to work out the value of y for $x = 2\frac{1}{2}$.)
(b) Where does the graph cut the x- and y-axes?
(c) Write down the equation for the line of symmetry of the graph.
(d) What is the minimum (least) value of $x^2 - 5x + 4$ (i.e. of y)? Which value of x gives the expression this minimum value? **11**

It is sometimes helpful to write a quadratic expression in the form $(x - h)^2 + k$. (This can always be done – sometimes h will be negative – and is useful for expressions that do not factorise.)
For example,

$$x^2 - 5x + 4 = (x - 2\tfrac{1}{2})^2 + \text{something},$$

(remember that $(x - h)^2 = x^2 - 2hx + \ldots$)
and by multiplying out $(x - 2\frac{1}{2})^2$ $[= x^2 - 5x + 6\frac{1}{4}]$ we see that the 'something' is $^-2\frac{1}{4}$.

Hence $$x^2 - 5x + 4 = (x - 2\tfrac{1}{2})^2 - 2\tfrac{1}{4}.$$

The minimum value of $(\text{anything})^2$ is zero. Hence the minimum value of $x^2 - 5x + 4$ [i.e. of $(x - 2\frac{1}{2})^2 - 2\frac{1}{4}$] is $0 - 2\frac{1}{4}$, or $^-2\frac{1}{4}$, and this occurs when $x - 2\frac{1}{2} = 0$, i.e. when $x = {}^+2\frac{1}{2}$. Compare these results with your answers to part (d) of question 4 above.

5 (a) Write the expression $x^2 + 2x - 8$ in the forms $(x + s)(x + t)$ and $(x - h)^2 + k$.
(b) Draw the graph of $y = x^2 + 2x - 8$ for values of x from $^{-}5$ to $^{+}3$.
(c) Write down the equation for the line of symmetry of the graph.
(d) State the value of x for which the expression has its minimum value; and write down this minimum value. 12

Exercise C

For questions 1 to 3 do the following.

(a) Compile a table of values of y for $^{-}4 \leqslant x \leqslant {}^{+}4$.
(b) Draw the graph.
(c) Write down the equation for the line of symmetry, and the coordinates of the 'turning point' (i.e. the point at which the function has its maximum or minimum value).

1 $y = x^2 - 2x - 4$

2 $y = 10 - x^2$

3 $y = \frac{1}{4}(x^2 - 4x + 5)$ 13

4 Rewrite the functions in questions 1 to 3 in the form $y = (x - h)^2 + k$, and hence write down the coordinates of the turning points. Compare with your answers above.

5 Describe, as fully as possible, the combination of transformations that would map the graph of $y = x^2$ onto each of the graphs that you have drawn for questions 1 to 3. 14

1.4 Quadratic equations

A quadratic equation has the form $ax^2 + bx + c = 0$, where a, b and c are given numbers. The solutions, or roots, of a quadratic equation are those values of x for which the value of $ax^2 + bx + c$ is zero. A quadratic equation cannot have more than two solutions; if it has just one solution then that solution is said to be a repeated root. Some quadratic equations have no (real) solutions, for example there is no value of x for which $3x^2 + 4 = 0$.

Some of the methods for solving such equations are as follows.

(1) By drawing a graph,
(2) by factorisation,
(3) by an iterative process (see Chapter 2),
(4) by 'completing the square' or by using a formula. (These methods do not have to be known for this course; an example of each will be found in questions 3 and 4 of Exercise D but otherwise they are not used.)

Graphical solution

To solve the equation $ax^2 + bx + c = 0$ we draw the graph of the function $y = ax^2 + bx + c$, and find the x-coordinates of the point or points for which the value of y is zero; i.e. we find the x-coordinates of the points where the curve crosses the line $y = 0$ (the x-axis).

Example 6. Solve graphically the equation $x^2 - x - 3 = 0$.

Figure 7 shows the graph of $y = x^2 - x - 3$, for $^{-}2 \leqslant x \leqslant 3$.

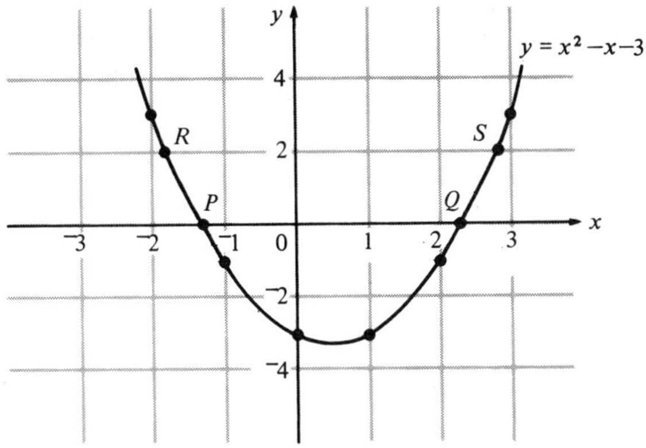

Figure 7

The points on this curve at which $y = 0$ are P and Q; the x-coordinates of these points are the values of x for which $x^2 - x - 3 = 0$.

The approximate solutions of the equation are therefore $x = {}^{-}1.3$, and $x = {}^{+}2.3$.

Note that once the graph in Figure 7 has been drawn it can be used also to solve equations such as $x^2 - x - 5 = 0$ (i.e. $x^2 - x - 3 = 2$) by finding the x-coordinates of the points where the curve crosses the line $y = 2$. These points are lettered R and S on Figure 7. This suggests that an alternative way of solving the equation $x^2 - x - 3 = 0$ would be to draw a simpler curve, such as $y = x^2 - x$ (i.e. $y = x(x - 1)$), and find the x-coordinates of the points where this curve crosses the line $y = 3$.

▷ 1 (a) Use your calculator to check that, when $x = {}^{-}1.3$ or ${}^{+}2.3$ the value of $x^2 - x - 3$ is approximately zero.

(b) From Figure 7 write down the solutions of $x^2 - x - 5 = 0$. Check your results with a calculator.

(c) Solve the equation $x^2 - x - 3 = 0$ by drawing the graph of $y = x^2 - x$ for values of x between $^{-}3$ and $^{+}3$ and finding the x-coordinates of the points where this curve crosses the line $y = 3$.

2 Draw the graph of $y = 4 + 3x - x^2$ for $^{-}2 \leqslant x \leqslant 5$, and hence solve the equation $4 + 3x - x^2 = 0$.

15

▷ 3 (a) Draw the graph of $y = x^2 - 3x + 2\frac{1}{4}$ for $0 \leqslant x \leqslant 4$.
What can you deduce about the solutions of the equation $x^2 - 3x + 2\frac{1}{4} = 0$?

(b) Repeat part (a) for the function $y = x^2 - 4x + 5$, and the equation $x^2 - 4x + 5 = 0$.

16

From these results it is clear that a quadratic equation $ax^2 + bx + c = 0$ may have two solutions, one solution, or no solutions; depending on whether the graph of the function $y = ax^2 + bx + c$ crosses, touches, or does not meet, the x-axis (i.e. the line $y = 0$).

Solution by factorisation

If the product of two numbers M and N is zero, what–if anything–can be said about the numbers M and N? Try multiplying several pairs of numbers together. When is the answer zero?

You should realise that if $M \times N = 0$, then either M itself is zero, or N itself is zero. Conversely, if either of M or N is zero, then the product $M \times N$ will also be zero. These results can be written as

$$M \times N = 0 \Leftrightarrow M = 0 \quad \text{or} \quad N = 0.$$

(This is read as 'the product of M and N is zero if, and only if, one of M or N is itself zero'.)

4 (a) If $5x = 0$, what can you say about the value of x?
(b) If $4(x - 3) = 0$, what can you say about the value of $(x - 3)$ and hence the value of x?
(c) If $xy = 0$, what can you say about the values of x and y? 17

Example 7. Solve the equation $x^2 + 5x - 24 = 0$.

The equation may be written as $(x + 8)(x - 3) = 0$,
hence either $x + 8 = 0$, or $x - 3 = 0$.
Thus either $x = {}^-8$, or $x = 3$.
The two solutions of the equation are $x = {}^-8$, and $x = 3$.

Example 8. Solve the equation $4x^2 + 11x = 0$.
Writing the equation as $x(4x + 11) = 0$,
we see that either $x = 0$, or $4x + 11 = 0$.
Thus the solutions are $x = 0$, and $x = {}^-2\frac{3}{4}$.

This method of solution is known as *solving by factorisation.*

5 Solve the following equations by factorisation.
(a) $x^2 - 7x + 6 = 0$ (b) $x^2 - 9x = 0$
(c) $20 - x - x^2 = 0$ (d) $9 - x^2 = 0$ 18

Exercise D

In each of the following questions solve the equation $8x^2 + 2x - 15$ by the method indicated.

1 (a) Draw the graph of $y = 8x^2 + 2x - 15$ for the following values of x.
${}^-2$, ${}^-1\frac{1}{2}$, ${}^-1$, ${}^-\frac{1}{2}$, 0, $\frac{1}{2}$, 1, $1\frac{1}{2}$, 2.
(b) Hence solve the equation, giving the solutions correct to one decimal place.

2 (a) Question 1 suggests that $x = {}^-1\frac{1}{2}$ is one solution of the equation. What is the corresponding factor of the expression $8x^2 + 2x - 15$?
(b) Find the other factor of the expression, and hence solve the equation by factorisation.

3* (Completing the square)

(a) Find values for g, h and k such that

$$8x^2 + 2x - 15 = 2(gx - h)^2 - k \text{ for all values of } x.$$

(b) Hence write the equation in the form $(gx - h)^2 = \frac{1}{2}k$.

(c) Solve this equation by using the flow diagram

$\frac{1}{2}k$ → [TAKE THE SQUARE ROOT] → [ADD h] → [DIVIDE BY g] → x

giving the solution(s) correct to two decimal places. Does this method give both solutions?

4* A formula for solving the quadratic equation $ax^2 + bx + c = 0$, based on the method of question 3, is

$$x = \frac{-b \pm \sqrt{(b^2 - 4ac)}}{2a}.$$

(a) What are the values of a, b and c for the equation of this exercise?

(b) Use these values in the formula above, and hence find the solutions of the equation.

*See the note at the beginning of Section 1.4.
A solution based on an iterative method will be found in Chapter 2.

19

Summary

(1) The distributive law for multiplication over addition (for real numbers) gives the expansions

$$a(b + c) = ab + ac,$$
$$(p + q)(r + s) = pr + ps + qr + qs.$$

These expansions are sometimes called 'multiplying out the brackets'.

(2) Some special examples of the above expansions are

$$(a + b)^2 = a^2 + 2ab + b^2$$
$$(a - b)^2 = a^2 - 2ab + b^2$$
$$(a + b)(a - b) = a^2 - b^2.$$

(3) Factorisation is the reverse of multiplying out the brackets.

(a) Expressions containing two terms are factorised as

either $ab + ac = a(b + c)$ (a is the common factor),
or $x^2 - y^2 = (x + y)(x - y)$ (the difference of two squares).

(b) Expressions of the form $x^2 + px + q$ can sometimes be factorised as $(x + s)(x + t)$, provided that we can find two numbers s and t such that $s + t = p$, and $s \times t = q$, taking due care with the plus and minus signs.

For example:
$$x^2 + 7x + 12 = x^2 + (3 + 4)x + 12 = (x + 3)(x + 4),$$
$$x^2 - 8x + 12 = x^2 - (6 + 2)x + 12 = (x - 6)(x - 2),$$
$$x^2 + 11x - 12 = x^2 + (12 - 1)x - 12 = (x + 12)(x - 1).$$

(4) An expression of the form $ax^2 + bx + c$ that contains a term in x^2, but no higher power of x, is called quadratic. The numbers a, b and c are called coefficients; a is the coefficient of x^2, etc.

(5) A quadratic function is of the form $f\colon x \to ax^2 + bx + c$ or $y = ax^2 + bx + c$.

The graph of a quadratic function is called a parabola.

Figure 8 shows the graph of $y = 4x^2 + 8x - 5$. This function may also be written in the forms $y = (2x - 1)(2x + 5)$ and $y = 4(x + 1)^2 - 9$. Figure 8 shows the connection between the coefficients in these alternative expressions and various points on the graph.

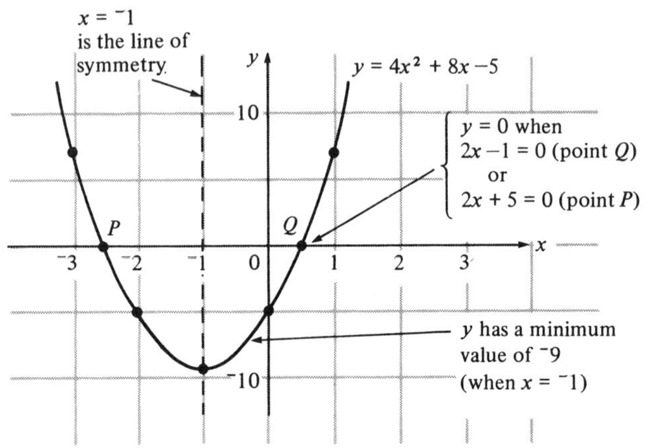

Figure 8

(6) A quadratic equation is of the form $ax^2 + bx + c = 0$. Such equations may have two solutions, one solution, or no solution.

Two methods of solving these equations are as follows.

(a) By drawing a graph.
From Figure 8 the solutions of the equation $4x^2 + 8x - 5 = 0$ are given by the x-coordinates of the points (P and Q) where the graph of $y = 4x^2 + 8x - 5$ crosses the line $y = 0$.

(b) By factorisation.
If two numbers M and N are such that $M \times N = 0$, then either M, or N, is itself zero.

Hence, since		$4x^2 + 8x - 5$	$=$	$(2x + 5)(2x - 1)$,
if		$4x^2 + 8x - 5$	$=$	0,
then		$(2x + 5)(2x - 1)$	$=$	0,
and so	either	$2x + 5 = 0$,	or	$2x - 1 = 0$,
i.e.	either	$x = {}^{-}2\frac{1}{2}$,	or	$x = \frac{1}{2}$.

Post-test

1 Multiply out the following.

(a) $(4x + 3)y$ (b) $(k + 7)(x - y)$ (c) $(5 + x)^2$

(d) $(2y - 3)^2$ (e) $(2p + 3q)(2p - 3q)$ (f) $(2 + 3z)(3 - 2z)$

2 Factorise the following.
(a) $6g - 12$ (b) $5x^2 - 10xy$ (c) $xy^2 - 4xz^2$
(d) $x^2 + 2x - 24$ (e) $m^2 - 13m + 30$ (f) $12 - q - q^2$
(g) $6x^2 + 13x - 5$, given that $(3x - 1)$ is one factor

3 (a) Express $x^2 - 2x - 8$ in factor form, and in the form $(x - h)^2 + k$.
(b) Draw the graph of $y = x^2 - 2x - 8$ for $^-3 \leqslant x \leqslant 5$.
(c) State the minimum value of $x^2 - 2x - 8$, the line of symmetry of the graph, and the solutions of the equation $x^2 - 2x - 8 = 0$.

4 Without drawing their graphs, solve the following equations where possible; stating whether the roots are integers, rational or irrational numbers, or explaining why no real roots are possible.
(a) $(x + 3)(2x - 5) = 0$ (b) $(x - 1)^2 - 25 = 0$
(c) $x^2 + 5 = 0$ (d) $x^2 - 5 = 0$ 20

Assignment

1 Multiply out the following.
(a) $(p + 2q)(3r + 4s)$ (b) $(1 + 2x - y)(x + 5y)$
(c) $(x + y - z)(x - y + z)$

2 Factorise the following.
(a) $\pi r^2 h + 2\pi rh$ (b) $60 + 23t + t^2$ (c) $x^2 + 4x + 4 - 9y^2$

3 (a) Solve the equation $9x - 2x^2 = 0$.
(b) Draw the graph of $y = 9x - 2x^2$ for $0 \leqslant x \leqslant 5$.
(c) From your graph find the maximum value of $9x - 2x^2$.

4 Solve the following equations.
(a) $4x^2 - 21x + 20 = 0$, given that one root is an integer
(b) $x^2 + 10x + q = (x + p)^2$ (c) $2 - 5x - 3x^2 = 0$

Answers

Pre-test

1 1 (a) $6x + 15$ (b) $2y + xy$ (c) $3 - 6x$
(d) $8x - 12xy$ (e) $1 - 3x - 6y$ (f) $5x + 5y - 6x - 15y = -x - 10y$

2 (a) $Q = 2x^2 + (^-3)x + 4 = 2x^2 - 3x + 4$
(b) When $x = 2$, $Q = 2(2)^2 - 3(2) + 4 = 8 - 6 + 4 = 6$
(c) When $x = {}^-2$, $Q = 2(^-2)^2 - 3(^-2) + 4 = 8 + 6 + 4 = 18$
(d) $Q = x^2 + 5x - 2$
When $x = 2$, $Q = 4 + 10 - 2 = 12$; when $x = {}^-2$, $Q = 4 - 10 - 2 = {}^-8$

3 See Figure A.

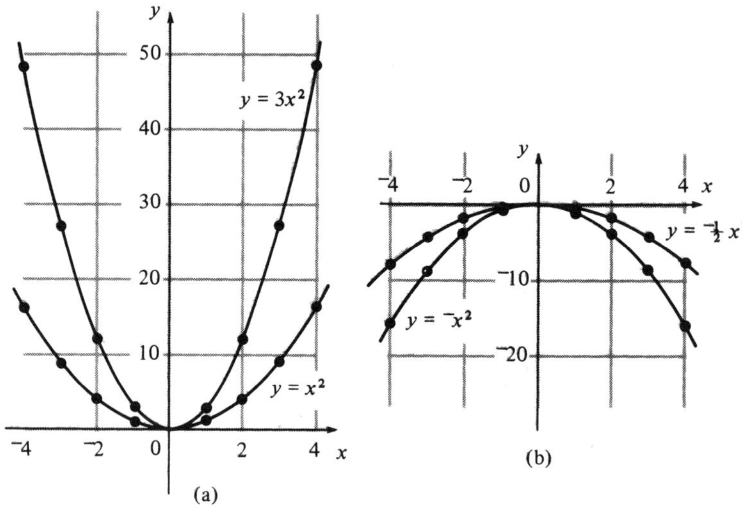

Figure A

4 (a)

x	$^{-}2$	$^{-}1$	0	$\frac{1}{2}$	1	$1\frac{1}{2}$	2	3	4	5
$f(x)$	5	0	$^{-}3$	$^{-}3\frac{3}{4}$	$^{-}4$	$^{-}3\frac{3}{4}$	$^{-}3$	0	5	12

(b) See Figure B. (Notice that after the table has been completed for part (a) we can see that we do not require to plot a point corresponding to $x = 5$ if we are looking only at what happens for small values of $f(x)$.)

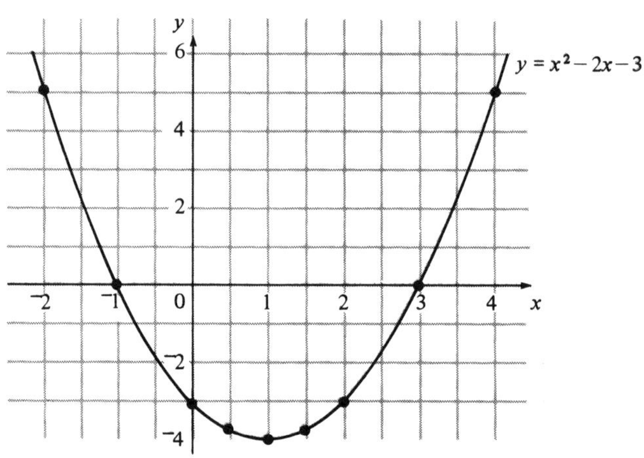

Figure B

(c) From the table, or from the graph, $f(x) = 0$ when $x = {}^{-}1$, and when $x = 3$.

1.1 The distributive law

2 **1** (a) $6(12+\frac{1}{2}) = 72 + 3 = 75$ (b) $37(100 + 0.2) = 3700 + 7.4 = 3707.4$
(c) $3x + 21$ (d) $12x - 20$ (e) $12x - 18y$
(f) $9x + hx$ (g) $5\frac{1}{2} + 3x$ (h) $8xz + 12yz$
(The second term in (f) could have been written as xh; it is more usual to write the factors of a product in alphabetical order.)

2 (a) $2 + 12 = 14$; $5 \times 6 = 30$
This shows that addition is **not** distributive over multiplication.
(b) $12 \div 6 = 2$; $6 + 3 = 9$
Division is **not** distributive over addition (from the left).
(c) $6 \div 12 = \frac{1}{2}$; $\frac{1}{6} + \frac{1}{3} = \frac{1}{2}$
This suggests, however, that division **is** distributive over addition from the right.

3 **3** (a) $(90 + 1)(80 + 1) = 7200 + 90 + 80 + 1 = 7371$
(b) $(20 - 1)(40 + 1) = 800 + 20 - 40 - 1 = 779$
(c) $(100 + 1)(100 - 1) = 10\,000 - 100 + 100 - 1 = 9999$

4 (a) $xy + 5x + 2y + 10$ (b) $x^2 + x + 3x + 3 = x^2 + 4x + 3$
(c) $x^2 + 4x - 3x - 12 = x^2 + x - 12$ (d) $yx - 5y + 6x - 30 = xy + 6x - 5y - 30$
(e) $x^2 - 8x - 7x + 56 = x^2 - 15x + 56$ (f) $xy - 2x - 2y + 4$

5 (a) $6xy + 8x + 3y + 4$ (b) $2x^2 + 10x + 3x + 15 = 2x^2 + 13x + 15$
(c) $15x^2 + 38x + 24$ (d) $6xy + 8x - 3y - 4$
(e) $2x^2 - 10x + 3x - 15 = 2x^2 - 7x - 15$ (f) $15x^2 - 38x + 24$

4 **6** (a) $x^2 + 4x + 4x + 16 = x^2 + 8x + 16$ (b) $9x^2 + 30x + 25$
(c) $4 + 36x + 81x^2$ (d) $x^2 - 4x - 4x + 16 = x^2 - 8x + 16$
(e) $9x^2 - 30x + 25$ (f) $4 - 36x + 81x^2$

7 (a) $x^2 - 7x + 7x - 49 = x^2 - 49$ (b) $4x^2 - 9$ (c) $16 - 9x^2$

8 (a) $(50 + 1)(50 + 1) = 2500 + 50 + 50 + 1 = 2601$
(b) $(50 - 1)(50 + 1) = 2500 + 50 - 50 - 1 = 2499$
(c) $(50 - 1)(50 - 1) = 2500 - 50 - 50 + 1 = 2401$

Exercise A

5 **1** (a) $2x$ (b) $1x$ (or just x)
(c) The product of $(x - 2)$ and $(x - 1)$ is the unshaded rectangle in Figure 5(c). This is obtained by taking away from the original rectangle the shaded parts of Figure 5(a) and Figure 5(b) in succession. But, before the second shaded rectangle can be subtracted, an extra 2×1 rectangle has to be added to the original. Hence

$$(x - 2)(x - 1) = x^2 + 2 - 2x - x = x^2 - 3x + 2.$$

2 See Figure C.

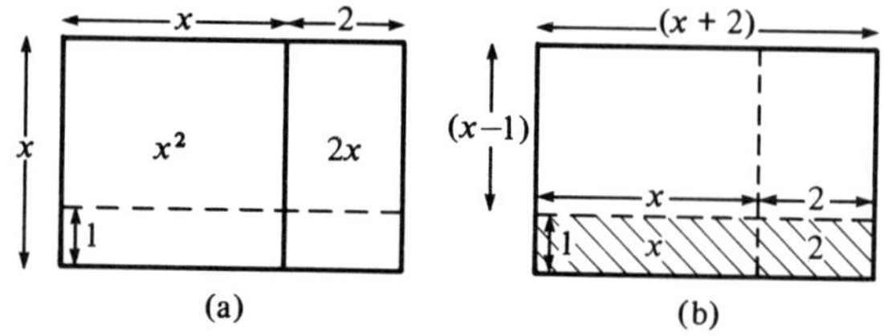

Figure C

The unshaded rectangle in Figure C(b) represents $(x + 2)(x - 1)$. Hence

$$(x+2)(x-1) = x^2 + 2x - 1x - 1 \times 2 = x^2 + x - 2.$$

3 (a) $x^2 + 8x + 12$ (b) $x^2 + 4x - 12$
(c) $x^2 - 4x - 12$ (d) $x^2 - 8x + 12$

4 (a) $6xy + 21x + 8y + 28$ (b) $6x^2 + 21x - 8x - 28 = 6x^2 + 13x - 28$
(c) $6xy - 21x + 8y - 28$ (d) $6x^2 - 21x - 8x + 28 = 6x^2 - 29x + 28$

5 (a) $x^2 + 2xy + y^2$ (b) $x^2 - 2xy + y^2$ (c) $x^2 - y^2$
(d) $x^2 - y^2$ (e) $p^2 + 2pq + q^2$ (f) $p^2 - 2pq + q^2$
(g) $q^2 - 2qp + p^2$ (i.e. $p^2 - 2pq + q^2$)
(h) $pq - p^2 + q^2 - qp = q^2 - p^2$ (or $-p^2 + q^2$)
(Note that $qp = pq$, therefore $pq - qp = 0$.)

6 (a) $9x^2 + 24x + 16$ (b) $9x^2 - 24x + 16$ (c) $9x^2 - 16$
(d) $9x^2 - 16$ (e) $16 - 24x + 9x^2$ (i.e. the same as (b))
(f) $12x + 16 - 9x^2 - 12x = 16 - 9x^2$

1.2 Factorisation

6 1 (a) $4(y + 3)$ (b) $3(1 - 8y)$ (c) $8(3x + 5y)$
(d) $x(x + 3y)$ (e) $3y(x - 4z)$ (f) $10(1 - z)$ (g) $z(z - 3)$

7 2 (a) $(x + q)(x - q)$ (b) $(x + 2p)(x - 2p)$ (c) $(3t + 1)(3t - 1)$
(d) $(6 + u)(6 - u)$ (e) $(4x + 5z)(4x - 5z)$ (f) $10(m + 2n)(m - 2n)$
(g) $25b(a + 2c)(a - 2c)$

8 3 (a) $x^2 + 3x + 2x + 6 = x^2 + 5x + 6$
(b) $x^2 - 3x + 2x - 6 = x^2 - x - 6$
(c) $x^2 + 3x - 2x - 6 = x^2 + x - 6$
(d) $x^2 - 3x - 2x + 6 = x^2 - 5x + 6$

4 (a) $x^2 + tx + sx + st = x^2 + (s + t)x + st$
(b) $s + t = 11$; $st = 24$
(c) $s = 3$, $t = 8$ (or vice versa)

Exercise B

9 **1** (a) $x^2 + 7x + 12 = (x + 3)(x + 4)$
(b) $x^2 + 10x - 24 = (x + 12)(x - 2)$

2 (a) $4(4 + b)$ (b) $d(d + 3bc)$ (c) $g(5 - h)$
(d) $3d(1 + 9d)$ (e) $2b(a + 3c - 6ac)$ (f) $(s + 8t)(s - 8t)$
(g) $2(7k + 5mn)(7k - 5mn)$ (h) $(x - 2)(x - 6)$
(i) $(x + 8)(x - 2)$ (j) $(x - 8)(x + 5)$
(Note that in question 1, and question 2 parts (f) to (j), the *order of the brackets* may be reversed, so that, for example, $(x + 5)(x - 8)$ is also a correct answer for 2(j); but the *numbers* cannot be interchanged: $(x - 5)(x + 8)$ is not a correct answer for 2(j).)

3 (a) $(x - 5)^2$ (b) $(2x + 5)^2$ (c) $(x + 13)(x - 13)$

4 (a) $(x - 5)$ (b) $(x - 2)$ (c) $(3x - 1)$ (d) $(4x - 3)$

1.3 Quadratic functions

10 **1** See Figure D.

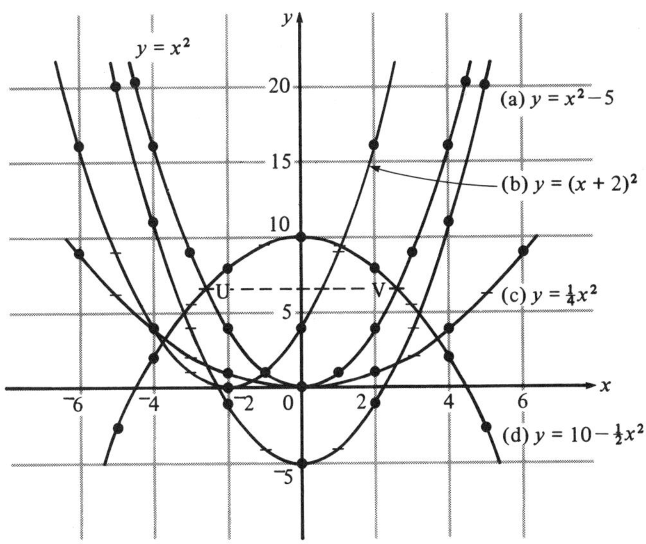

Figure D

2 The values for y are as follows.
(a) 20, 11, $^-1$, $^-5$, $^-1$, 11, 20
(b) 16, 4, 0, 4, 16
(c) 9, 4, 1, 0, 1, 4, 9
(d) $^-2\frac{1}{2}$, 2, 8, 10, 8, 2, $^-2\frac{1}{2}$
The detailed calculations for $x = {}^-4$ are as follows.
(a) $(^-4)^2 - 5 = 16 - 5 = 11$ (b) $(^-4 + 2)^2 = (^-2)^2 = 4$
(c) $\frac{1}{4}(^-4)^2 = \frac{1}{4}(16) = 4$ (d) $10 - \frac{1}{2}(^-4)^2 = 10 - \frac{1}{2}(16) = 2$
The graphs of these functions are shown in Figure D.

3 (a) $y = x^2 \rightarrow y = x^2 - 5$: translation $\begin{bmatrix} 0 \\ ^-5 \end{bmatrix}$.

(b) $y = x^2 \rightarrow y = (x+2)^2$: translation $\begin{bmatrix} ^-2 \\ 0 \end{bmatrix}$.

(c) $y = x^2 \rightarrow y = \frac{1}{4}x^2$: various transformations are possible, such as
one-way stretch from $x = 0$, scale factor 2: $(1, 1) \rightarrow (2, 1)$,
one-way stretch from $y = 0$, scale factor $\frac{1}{4}$: $(1, 1) \rightarrow (1, \frac{1}{4})$,
enlargement from the origin, scale factor 4: $(1, 1) \rightarrow (4, 4)$.

(d) $y = x^2 \rightarrow y = 10 - \frac{1}{2}x^2$; various combinations are possible. A reflection in $y = 0$ followed by a translation of $\begin{bmatrix} 0 \\ 10 \end{bmatrix}$; or a translation of $\begin{bmatrix} 0 \\ 10 \end{bmatrix}$ followed by a reflection in $y = 10$; or a reflection in $y = 5$ will all map the original onto $y = 10 - x^2$. The final stage could be a one-way stretch from $y = 10$ with scale factor $\frac{1}{2}$, a one-way stretch from $x = 0$ with scale factor $\sqrt{2}$, or an enlargement from (0, 10) with scale factor 2. Perhaps the neatest transformation is a one-way stretch from the line $y = 6\frac{2}{3}$ (the line UV on Figure D) with scale factor of $^-\frac{1}{2}$.

11 4 (a) When $x = 2\frac{1}{2}$ the value of $y = (2\frac{1}{2} - 1)(2\frac{1}{2} - 4) = (1\frac{1}{2})(^-1\frac{1}{2}) = {}^-2\frac{1}{4}$. The graph is shown in Figure E.

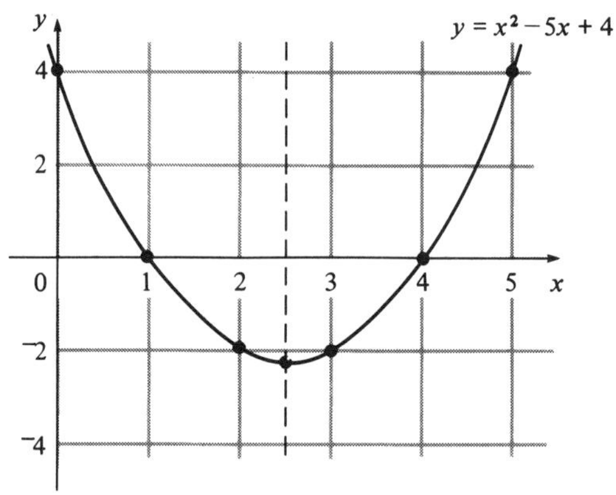

Figure E

(b) The graph cuts the x-axis at the points where $x = 1$ and $x = 4$, and it cuts the y-axis at the point where $y = 4$.
If the equation can be written as $y = (x - a)(x - b)$, then the curve cuts the x-axis at the points for which $x = a$ and $x = b$. When the equation is written in the form $y = ax^2 + bx + c$, the constant term (c) gives the y-coordinate of the point where the curve cuts the y-axis.

(c) The line of symmetry is $x = 2\frac{1}{2}$.

(d) The least value of y is $^-2\frac{1}{4}$. This is given by $x = 2\frac{1}{2}$.
(In other words, the greatest or least value of a quadratic expression is given by the point where the line of symmetry meets the curve.)

12 5 (a) $x^2 + 2x - 8 = (x + 4)(x - 2) = (x + 1)^2 - 9$

(b) The table of values is

x	$^-5$	$^-4$	$^-3$	$^-2$	$^-1$	0	1	2	3
y	7	0	$^-5$	$^-8$	$^-9$	$^-8$	$^-5$	0	7

The graph is shown in Figure F.

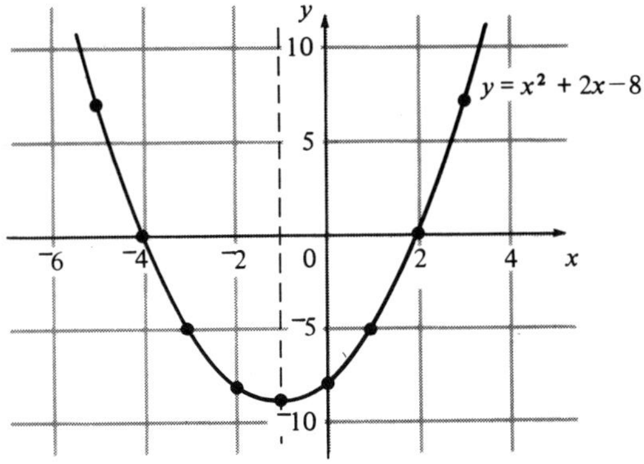

Figure F

(c) and (d) The second form of the expression also tells us that the minimum value of y is $^{-}9$, which occurs when $x = {}^{-}1$, and that the line of symmetry of the curve is $x = {}^{-}1$.

Exercise C

13 1 $y = x^2 - 2x - 4$

(a) x	$^{-}4$	$^{-}3$	$^{-}2$	$^{-}1$	0	1	2	3	4
y	20	11	4	$^{-}1$	$^{-}4$	$^{-}5$	$^{-}4$	$^{-}1$	4

(b) See Figure G.

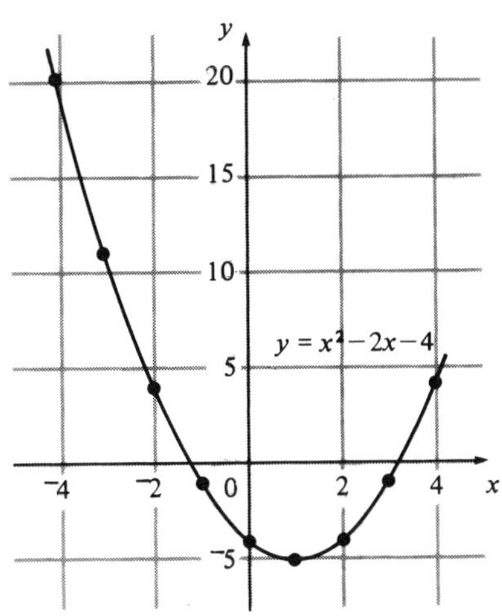

Figure G

(c) Line of symmetry is $x = 1$. Turning point is $(1, {}^{-}5)$.

2 $y = 10 - x^2$

(a)

x	$^-4$	$^-3$	$^-2$	$^-1$	0	1	2	3	4
y	$^-6$	1	6	9	10	9	6	1	$^-6$

(b) See Figure H.

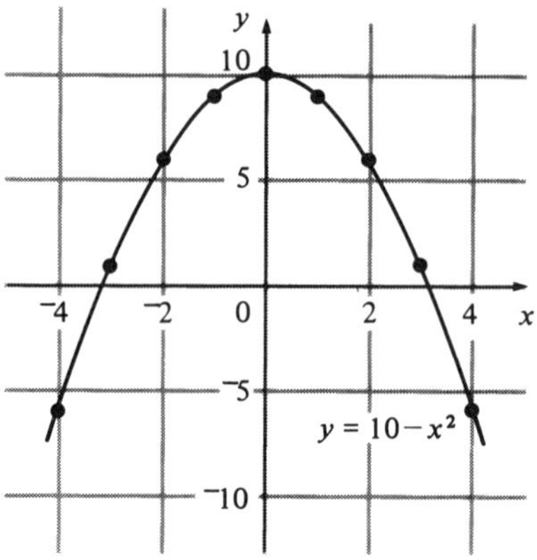

Figure H

(c) Line of symmetry is $x = 0$. Turning point is $(0, 10)$.

3 $y = \frac{1}{4}(x^2 - 4x + 5)$

(a)

x	$^-4$	$^-3$	$^-2$	$^-1$	0	1	2	3	4
y	$9\frac{1}{4}$	$6\frac{1}{2}$	$4\frac{1}{4}$	$2\frac{1}{2}$	$1\frac{1}{4}$	$\frac{1}{2}$	$\frac{1}{4}$	$\frac{1}{2}$	$1\frac{1}{4}$

(b) See Figure I.

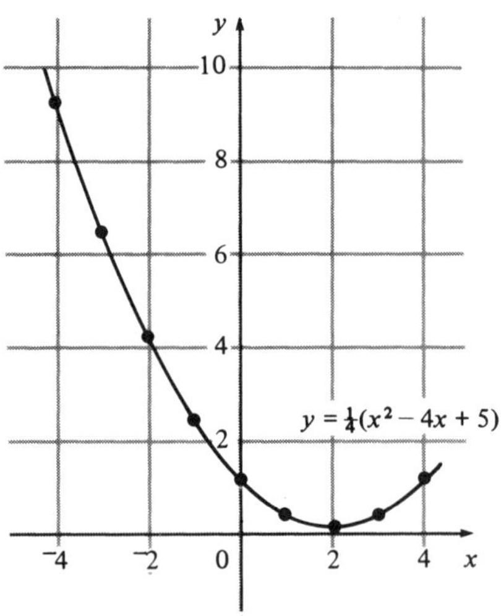

Figure I

(c) Line of symmetry is $x = 2$. Turning point is $(2, \frac{1}{4})$.

14 4 (a) $y = (x-1)^2 - 5$. Turning point is $(1, {}^{-}5)$.
(b) $y = -x^2 + 10$. Turning point is $(0, 10)$.
(Or $-(x-0)^2 + 10$. The minus sign shows that the curve is 'upside-down', i.e. the turning point is at the top.)
(c) $y = \frac{1}{4}[(x-2)^2 + 1] = \frac{1}{4}(x-2)^2 + \frac{1}{4}$. Turning point is $(2, \frac{1}{4})$.

5 (a) A translation of $\begin{bmatrix} 1 \\ -5 \end{bmatrix}$.

(b) Reflection in $y = 0$, followed by a translation of $\begin{bmatrix} 0 \\ 10 \end{bmatrix}$; or translation of $\begin{bmatrix} 0 \\ 10 \end{bmatrix}$, followed by reflection in $y = 10$; or reflection in $y = 5$.

(c) A combination, in either order, of a translation of $\begin{bmatrix} 2 \\ \frac{1}{4} \end{bmatrix}$ and a stretch or an enlargement. The latter could be one of an enlargement, centre at turning point, scale factor 4; a one-way stretch from the horizontal line through the turning point, scale factor $\frac{1}{4}$; a one-way stretch from the vertical line through the turning point, scale factor 2.

1.4 Quadratic equations

15 1 (a) If $f(x) = x^2 - x - 3$, then $f({}^{-}1.3) = {}^{-}0.01$ and $f(2.3) = {}^{-}0.01$.
(b) From Figure 7, $y = 2$ when $x = {}^{-}1.8$ and when $x = 2.8$ (approximately).
By calculation, when $x = {}^{-}1.8$ (or 2.8), $y = 2.04$, hence for these values of x the value of $x^2 - x - 5$ (i.e. of $y - 2$) is 0.04, and so these values of x are approximate solutions of the equation $x^2 - x - 5 = 0$.
(c) See Figure J.
The table of values is

x	$^{-}3$	$^{-}2$	$^{-}1$	0	1	2	3
y	12	6	2	0	0	2	6

From the graph, when $y = 3$, $x = {}^{-}1.3$ or 2.3. (Compare part (a).)

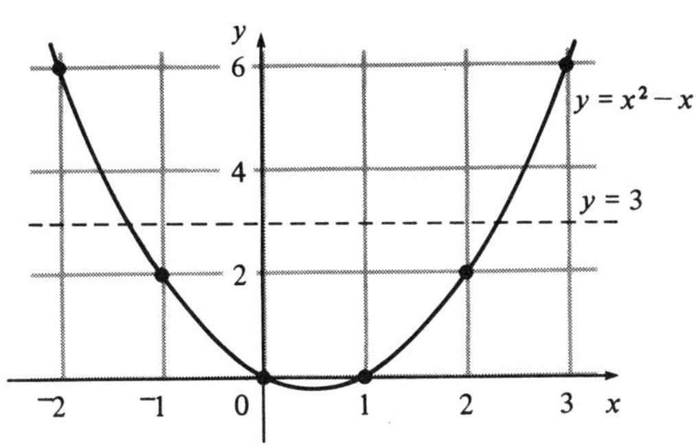

Figure J

2 See Figure K.

x	$^{-}2$	$^{-}1$	0	1	2	3	4	5
y	$^{-}6$	0	4	6	6	4	0	$^{-}6$

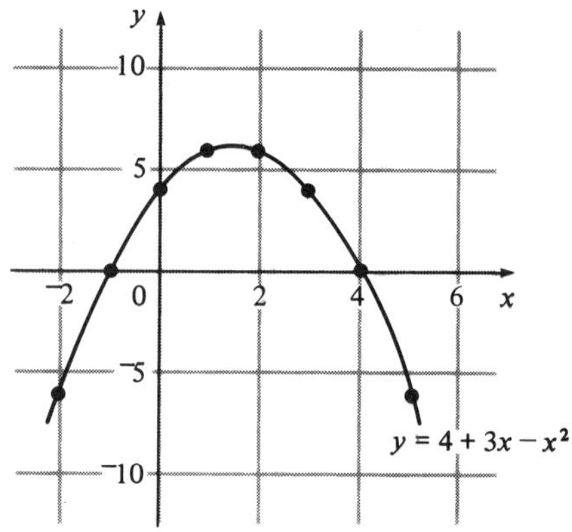

Figure K

$4 + 3x - x^2 = 0$ when $x = {}^{-}1$, and when $x = 4$.

16 3 (a) See Figure L(a).

x	0	1	2	3	4	$1\frac{1}{2}$
y	$2\frac{1}{4}$	$\frac{1}{4}$	$\frac{1}{4}$	$2\frac{1}{4}$	$6\frac{1}{4}$	0

From the table of values it is clear that the line of symmetry is $x = 1\frac{1}{2}$, and so the turning point of the graph will occur for this value of x. As $y = 0$ when $x = 1\frac{1}{2}$, the line $y = 0$ *touches* the curve at this point, and so there is only one solution to the equation $x^2 - 3x + 2\frac{1}{4} = 0$, namely $x = 1\frac{1}{2}$. (If the line $y = 0$ cuts a parabola at all, it usually does so in two distinct points. This is a 'limiting case' of such a situation, and the two points can be regarded as coinciding, hence the description 'repeated root'.)

(b) See Figure L(b)

x	0	1	2	3	4
y	5	2	1	2	5

The line of symmetry is $x = 2$. Hence the line $y = 0$ does not meet the curve, and so there are no values of x for which the value of $x^2 - 4x + 5$ is zero; i.e. the equation $x^2 - 4x + 5$ has no (real) solutions.

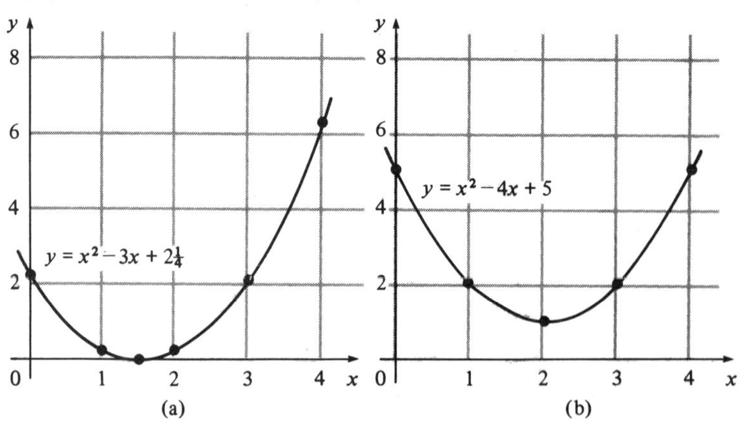

Figure L

17 **4** (a) As the product of 5 and x is zero, one of these two numbers must itself be zero. The number 5 cannot be zero, hence x must be zero.
(b) Similarly, $(x - 3)$ must be zero, hence $x = 3$.
(c) One of the two numbers (x and y) must be zero, but without further information we do not know which, and so we have to consider two possibilities. If, for example, we assume that $x = 0$ then y can have any value at this stage: it, also, could be zero—but it does not have to be.

18 **5** (a) Hence $(x - 6)(x - 1) = 0$. Either $x = 6$, or $x = 1$.
(b) $x(x - 9) = 0$. Either $x = 0$, or $x = 9$.
(c) $(5 + x)(4 - x) = 0$. Either $x = {}^-5$, or $x = 4$.
(d) $(3 + x)(3 - x) = 0$. Either $x = {}^-3$, or $x = 3$.

Exercise D

19 **1** (a) See Figure M.

x	$^-2$	$^-1\frac{1}{2}$	$^-1$	$^-\frac{1}{2}$	0	$\frac{1}{2}$	1	$1\frac{1}{2}$	2
y	13	0	$^-9$	$^-14$	$^-15$	$^-12$	$^-5$	6	21

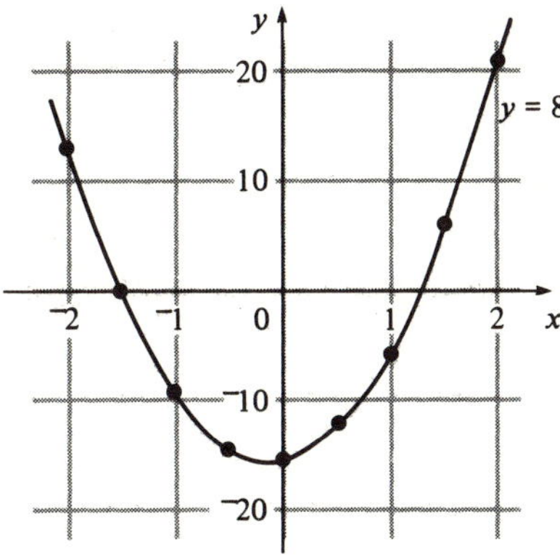

Figure M

(b) From the graph, $y = 0$ when $x = {}^-1.5$, and when $x = 1.2$ (or 1.3).

2 (a) The factor corresponding to $x = {}^-1\frac{1}{2}$ is $(x + 1\frac{1}{2})$ or $(2x + 3)$.
(b) Hence $8x^2 + 2x - 15 = (2x + 3)(\quad) = (2x + 3)(4x - 5)$.
The solutions of $8x^2 + 2x - 15 = 0$ are $x = {}^-1\frac{1}{2}$ and $x = 1\frac{1}{4}$.

3 (a) $8x^2 + 2x - 15 = 2(2x + \frac{1}{4})^2 - 15\frac{1}{8}$ (i.e. $g = 2$, $h = {}^-\frac{1}{4}$, $k = 15\frac{1}{8}$).
(b) Hence if $8x^2 + 2x - 15 = 0$,
then $2(2x + \frac{1}{4})^2 - 15\frac{1}{8} = 0$,
i.e. $(2x + \frac{1}{4})^2 = 7\frac{9}{16}$.
(c) The stages are

$7\frac{9}{16}$ (i.e. $\frac{121}{16}$) → $\pm\frac{11}{4}$ (i.e. $\pm 2\frac{3}{4}$) → $2\frac{1}{2}$ or $^-3$ → $1\frac{1}{4}$ or $^-1\frac{1}{2}$

or 7.56 → ± 2.75 → 2.5 or $^-3$ → 1.25 or $^-1.5$

Both solutions are given if you remember that a (positive) number has two square roots.

4 (a) For the equation $8x^2 + 2x - 15 = 0$, the values are $a = 8$, $b = 2$, and $c = {}^{-}15$.

(b) Substituting in the formula gives

$$x = \frac{-2 \pm \sqrt{[(2)^2 - 4(8)({}^{-}15)]}}{2(8)} = \frac{-2 \pm \sqrt{484}}{16} = \frac{-2 \pm 22}{16}.$$

Hence, either $x = \dfrac{-2+22}{16} = \dfrac{20}{16} = 1\tfrac{1}{4}$, or $x = \dfrac{-2-22}{16} = \dfrac{-24}{16} = {}^{-}1\tfrac{1}{2}$.

Post-test

20 **1** (a) $4xy + 3y$ (b) $kx - ky + 7x - 7y$ (c) $25 + 10x + x^2$ (or $x^2 + 10x + 25$)
(d) $4y^2 - 12y + 9$ (e) $4p^2 - 9q^2$ (f) $6 + 5z - 6z^2$ (or $-6z^2 + 5z + 6$)

2 (a) $6(g-2)$ (b) $5x(x-2y)$ (c) $x(y^2 - 4z^2) = x(y+2z)(y-2z)$
(d) $(x+6)(x-4)$ (e) $(m-10)(m-3)$ (f) $(4+q)(3-q)$
(g) $(3x-1)(2x+5)$

3 (a) $x^2 - 2x - 8 = (x+2)(x-4) = (x-1)^2 - 9$

(b) See Figure N.

x	$^{-}3$	$^{-}2$	$^{-}1$	0	1	2	3	4	5
y	7	0	$^{-}5$	$^{-}8$	$^{-}9$	$^{-}8$	$^{-}5$	0	7

(c) The minimum value of $x^2 - 2x - 8$ is $^{-}9$; the line of symmetry of the graph is $x = 1$; and the solutions of the equation are $x = {}^{-}2$, and $x = 4$.

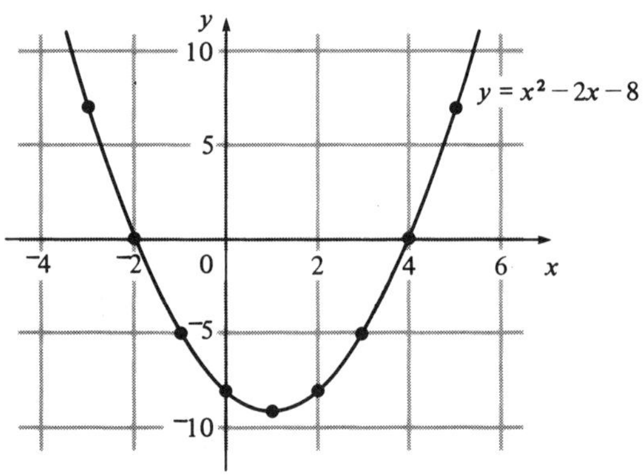

Figure N

4 (a) This equation can be solved by factorisation. The solutions are $x = {}^{-}3$, and $x = 2\tfrac{1}{2}$. One root is an integer, and the other is a rational number.

(b) This equation can be factorised to give $(x - 1 + 5)(x - 1 - 5) = 0$, giving two integral solutions, $x = {}^{-}4$ and $x = 6$.
Alternatively, the equation can be written as $(x-1)^2 = 25$.
Taking the square root of both sides gives
$x - 1 = \pm 5$; hence $x = 1 + 5$ (= 6), or $x = 1 - 5$ (= $^{-}4$).

(c) This equation has no solutions, as the minimum value of the expression $x^2 + 5$ is 5.

(d) This can be re-written as $x^2 = 5$. Taking the square root of both sides, we have $x = \pm\sqrt{5}$ (approximately ± 2.24), i.e. two irrational roots.

2 The calculator and flow diagrams

Objectives

This is what you should be able to do after studying this chapter.

(1) Use a calculator to find numerical solutions to problems, including those that can be solved by an iterative method.

(2) Interpret flow diagrams, and construct simple flow diagrams.

(3) Use a calculator in conjunction with a flow diagram.

Pre-test

1 Without using calculators, tables, or slide rules, evaluate (i.e. find the value of) the following.

(a) $9 \times 4 + 7$ (b) $9 \times (4 + 7)$ (c) $9 + 4 \times 7$ (d) $(9 + 4) \times 7$
(e) $12 + 4 \div 2$ (f) $(12 + 4) \div 2$ (g) $12 \div 4 + 2$ (h) $12 \div (4 + 2)$
(i) $3 + 5^2$ (j) $(3 + 5)^2$ (k) $(^-2) + (^-7)$ (l) $(^-2) - (^-7)$
(m) $(^-2) \times 7$ (n) $(^-2) \times (^-7)$ (o) $4 + (^-5)^2$ (p) $4 + {}^-(5^2)$
(q) $(18 \div 6) \div 3$ (r) $18 \div (6 \div 3)$ (s) $(10 \div 5) \times 2$ (t) $10 \div (5 \times 2)$

2 Calculate the volume of a sphere of radius 21 cm from the formula $V = \frac{4}{3}\pi r^3$, using the value $\frac{22}{7}$ for π.

3 (a) Use the flow diagram below to evaluate y when $x = 4$.

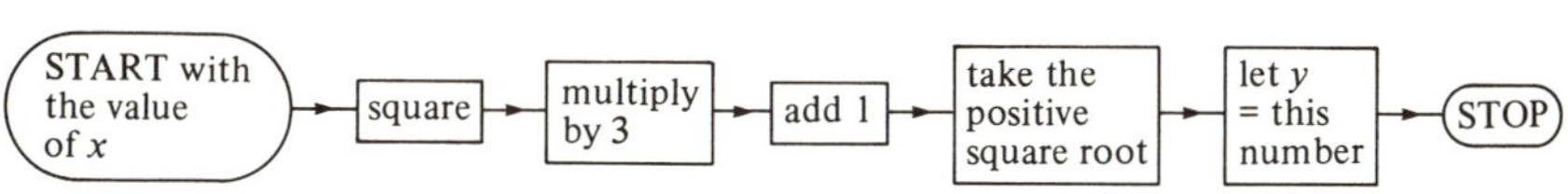

(b) Express y in terms of x.

4 Construct a flow diagram to evaluate A from the formula

$$A = 1000\left(1 + \frac{x}{100}\right)^3,$$

and find the value of A when $x = 20$.

2.1 Using a calculator

The range and diversity of calculators available at reasonable prices is increasing all the time, and so this section cannot instruct you in the use of any particular calculator. You must study the instructions carefully, until you become proficient in the use of your own calculator.

Make sure, for example, that you know the correct order for entering numbers and operations (+, –, ×, ÷, etc.). Most calculators use 'true algebraic logic' or 'algebraic operating system' in which, for example, the calculation of 3 + 5 is entered as

3, +, 5, =

but some calculators use 'reverse Polish notation' in which the order of entries is

3, 5, +

1 Check that you know how to use your calculator to obtain the correct answers to question 1 of the Pre-test.

2 Use a calculator to evaluate question 2 of the Pre-test
(a) using $\frac{22}{7}$ for π, (b) using 3.142 for π,
(c) using the button [π], or the value 3.141 593, for π. 2

Whenever you use a new function, or a new calculator, practise first with an easy example for which you already know the answer.

3 Suppose you are using the 'square root' button ([$\sqrt{x}$] or [$\sqrt{\ }$]) for the first time. 'Test' your calculator with the following.
(a) $\sqrt{144}$ (b) $\sqrt{14.4}$ (c) $\sqrt{1.44}$ (d) $\sqrt{0.144}$ (e) $\sqrt{0.0144}$
(f) $\sqrt{^{-}144}$ 3

Do you know what happens when your calculator 'overflows'?
(This means that either the answer has more digits in front of the decimal point than the number of figures that the calculator displays, or that the answer to the calculation exceeds 10^{100}.)

4 What answer does your calculator give for 123 456 × 7 891 011? 4

The exact answer has twelve significant figures in front of the decimal point. Very few calculators display this number of digits. Does your calculator put the answer into 'standard form' (scientific notation)? (See Chapter 1 of *Computation and Graphs*.) If so, it will probably display

9.74193 11

(which stands for 9.741 93 × 10^{11}) which is the answer correct to six significant figures.

If it does not have this facility, does the calculator tell you that it cannot cope – by displaying an 'overflow' symbol – or does it just display the first (or last) six, seven or eight significant figures (with or without the decimal point)? These last results are possible on some calculators!

5 (a) Use your calculator to evaluate 1.23×4.56.

(b) If your calculator uses standard form, make sure that you can enter and evaluate correctly

$$(1.23 \times 10^{14}) \times (4.56 \times 10^{25}).$$

(c) What result does your calculator give for

$$(1.23 \times 10^{67}) \times (4.56 \times 10^{89})?$$ 5

Some points to notice

(1) Always check that the answer given by the calculator is reasonable. Either before or after using the calculator, make an estimate of the size of the answer. (See Chapter 2 of *Computation and Graphs*.) You may have entered a decimal point in the wrong place!

(2) Perform the calculation a second time in a different order, or 'work backwards' from your original answer. Working backwards is especially useful when the result seems to be of the right order of magnitude, but you want to check that you have not miskeyed one figure, or made two errors that tend to cancel each other out.

Example 1. A student evaluated $\dfrac{3.75 \times 4.31}{11.46}$ as 14.4993.

Check: Since $3 \times 4 = 12$,

then $\dfrac{3 \times 4}{11}$ should give an answer between 1 and 2.

The student's answer is not correct!

Second calculation:

If the original calculation was performed in the order

3.75 → [× 4.31] → [÷ 11.46] → answer,

re-work the calculation in the order

3.75 → [÷ 11.46] → [× 4.31] → new answer.

and/or work backwards; for example

answer → [× 11.46] → [÷ 4.31] →

or answer → [÷ 4.31] → [× 11.46] →

should give a result of 3.75.

6 When the student re-worked the calculation in a different order the new answer was 1.41688. Use the two 'backwards' methods quoted above to find whether either of 1.44993 or 1.41688 is the correct answer.

If neither appears to be correct, work the question out for yourself – and check your answer! 6

(3) Consider the order in which you perform a calculation in relation to your machine.

For example, it is usually better to perform a calculation of the form $\dfrac{p \times q}{r}$ in the order

$$p \rightarrow \boxed{\times q} \rightarrow \boxed{\div r} \rightarrow$$

but if the product of p and q overflows then perform the calculation in the order

$$p \rightarrow \boxed{\div r} \rightarrow \boxed{\times q} \rightarrow$$

(and check by calculating $q \rightarrow \boxed{\div r} \rightarrow \boxed{\times p} \rightarrow$).

7 Evaluate the following. $\dfrac{(9.23 \times 10^{51}) \times (2.05 \times 10^{60})}{(5.55 \times 10^{43})}$ 7

(4) In written work (especially in examinations!) write down on paper the calculation that you are going to do; then use your calculator; write down the full result; correct the result to a suitable degree of accuracy.

Example 2. Calculate the volume of a sphere whose radius is 6.20 cm.
The following four lines should all be written down on paper.

$$\begin{aligned} \text{Volume of sphere} &= \tfrac{4}{3}\pi r^3 \\ &= \tfrac{4}{3} \times \pi \times (6.2)^3 \text{ cm}^3 \\ &= 998.305\,99 \text{ cm}^3 \text{ (by calculator)} \\ &= 998 \text{ cm}^3 \text{ (correct to 3 s.f.).} \end{aligned}$$

8 The volume (V cm^3) of a 'bobbing dunce' is given by the formula

$$V = \frac{\pi r^2 (2r + h)}{3}.$$

Calculate the volume when $r = 4.2$ (cm) and $h = 5.6$ (cm).
(Use the value 3.141 59 if your calculator does not have a $\boxed{\pi}$ button.) 8

(5) Accuracy. While you are working through a calculation you should use the full capacity of the machine, and any intermediate results that need to be written down should be recorded fully, and re-entered in full if required later. But the final answer should be rounded to a suitable degree of accuracy. Some guidelines on this will be found in Chapter 2 of *Computation and Graphs*.

Some examples involving accuracy will be found in Section 2.2.

Available functions

For this chapter it is assumed that your calculator has the basic 'functions' +, –, ×, ÷, a square root button, and a memory. It is also helpful, but by no means essential, to have a $\boxed{\pi}$ button, a square button ($\boxed{x^2}$), and a reciprocal button ($\boxed{\frac{1}{x}}$). If you are going to do much work involving trigonometry, the six trigonometrical buttons $\boxed{\text{sin}}$, $\boxed{\text{cos}}$, $\boxed{\text{tan}}$, $\boxed{\text{arcsin}}$ (or $\boxed{\text{sin}^{-1}}$), $\boxed{\text{arccos}}$, and $\boxed{\text{arctan}}$ can be useful.

If your calculator does not have a $\boxed{\pi}$ button use the value 3.141 593.

Exercise A

1 Use your calculator to evaluate the following.

(a) $$\frac{4 \times 2.5^2 + 11 \times 7.5^2 + 8 \times 12.5^2 + 2 \times 17.5^2}{25}$$

(b) $$\frac{1}{2.6^2 + 3.7^2} - \frac{1}{8.3^2 + 1.9^2}$$

2 The total surface area of a cone of height h cm and base radius r cm is given by the formula $A = \pi r(r + s)$, where $s^2 = r^2 + h^2$.
Calculate the total surface area of a cone of height 16.3 cm and base radius 7.5 cm.

3 The area (A cm^2) of a triangle whose sides are of lengths a cm, b cm and c cm is given by the formula

$$A = \sqrt{[s(s-a)(s-b)(s-c)]},$$

where $$s = \tfrac{1}{2}(a + b + c).$$

Calculate the area of a triangle whose sides are of lengths 8.3 cm, 5.7 cm and 12.1 cm.

9

2.2 Some applications

Limits of accuracy

In the previous section some guidelines for accuracy were stated. We shall now explore these a little further.

Example 3. The internal dimensions of a box are: length 28 cm, width 19 cm, and height 24 cm. Calculate its internal volume.

(a) If we assume that the measurements are exact there is little difficulty.

$$\begin{aligned} \text{Volume} &= \text{length} \times \text{width} \times \text{height} \\ &= 28\text{ cm} \times 19\text{ cm} \times 24\text{ cm} \\ &= 12\,768\text{ cm}^3. \end{aligned}$$

(b) But in practice these measurements will not be exact.
Suppose that they are correct to the nearest centimetre.
Then, for example, the internal length would be somewhere between $27\frac{1}{2}$ cm and $28\frac{1}{2}$ cm.

At one extreme the length could be as small as 27.5 cm, the width as small as 18.5 cm, and the height as small as 23.5 cm. These measurements would give a minimum value for the volume as

$$27.5\text{ cm} \times 18.5\text{ cm} \times 23.5\text{ cm} = 11\,955.625\text{ cm}^3.$$

At the other extreme, the maximum value of the volume would be

$$28.5\text{ cm} \times 19.5\text{ cm} \times 24.5\text{ cm} = 13\,615.875\text{ cm}^3.$$

From this example we can see that if the original dimensions are correct only to two significant figures, then the range of possible values for the volume is quite large.

Certainly the answer should not be given to any more than two significant figures; and even the two significant figure answer of 13 000 cm^3 would not always be correct. (Statistically it can be shown that if the dimensions are chosen at random within the limits stated, then about 20% of the combinations would give an answer of 12 000 cm^3 correct to two significant figures, and about $\frac{1}{2}$% of the combinations would give an answer of 14 000 cm^3 correct to two significant figures.)

1 The internal dimensions of a cereal packet are as follows:

length 20 cm, width 7 cm, height 29 cm.

(a) Calculate the internal volume of the packet, assuming all the measurements are exact.
(b) Calculate the maximum and minimum possible volumes, given that the measurements are correct to the nearest centimetre only.

2 Calculate the maximum and minimum volumes of the packet described in question 1 given that the measurements are correct
(a) to the nearest 2 mm;.
(b) to the nearest mm.
In each case, state the answer to an appropriate degree of accuracy.

10

Graphical work

It is sometimes necessary in graphical work to find where a graph crosses an axis (e.g. in solving an equation by a graphical method), or to estimate the gradient of a curve at a particular point (e.g. in finding the speed of an object from its distance–time graph). These topics are covered in *Algebra 2: Equations, Formulas and Graphs.*

If the equation of the graph or curve is known, this can be done numerically, as shown in the example below. (The algebraic development of these ideas is the basis of the branch of mathematics known as calculus.)

Example 4. Figure 1 shows part of the graph of the function

$$f: x \to x^3 - 3x^2 + 3.$$

Find the coordinates of P, and the gradient at Q, giving each answer correct to two decimal places.

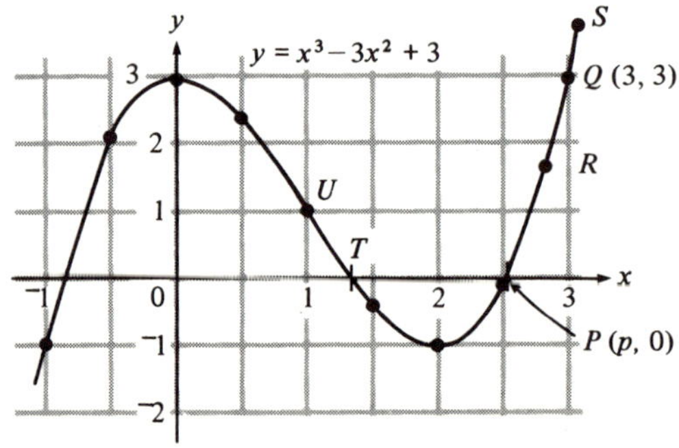

Figure 1

(a) To find the coordinates of P.
From the graph it is clear that $2 < p < 3$.
We use a calculator to evaluate $f(2.4)$, $f(2.5)$, $f(2.6)$, . . ., to find two closer limits.
(You may find it helpful to express $f(x)$ in the form

$$f\colon x \to x^2(x-3)+3.)$$

x	2.4	2.5	2.6
$f(x)$	⁻0.456	⁻0.125	0.296

We now have one negative value of $f(x)$ and one positive value; so we can now say that $2.5 < p < 2.6$, and, as $f(2.5)$ is numerically the smaller of the two, it is likely that p is nearer to 2.5 than to 2.6.

Repeat the process for $f(2.52)$ (say), $f(2.53)$, . . .

x	2.52	2.53	2.54
$f(x)$	⁻0.048	⁻0.008	0.032

(Only the first three decimal places of $f(x)$ have been written down, as they are sufficient to determine in which interval p lies.)
From this it is seen that p lies between 2.53 and 2.54, and is closer to 2.53.

Hence the coordinates of P are (2.53, 0), correct to two decimal places.

(b) To find the gradient at Q.
If R and S are two points on the curve close to, but on opposite sides of, the point Q, then the gradient at Q will be less steep than the gradient of QS, but steeper than the gradient of QR.

We calculate the gradients of QR and QS for points R and S closer and closer to Q, until we can limit our range of values for the gradient at Q to any required degree of accuracy.

If the x-coordinate of R is $x = r$, then the y-coordinate will be $y = f(r)$, and the gradient of QR is

$$\frac{f(3)-f(r)}{3-r} \quad \text{(see Figure 2).}$$

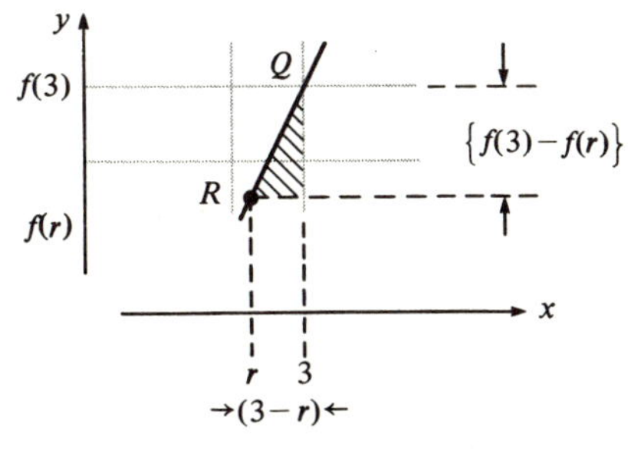

Figure 2

There is no hard and fast rule for what values of r (and s) to take so that the points R and S become closer to Q. One technique is illustrated below.

r	$f(r)$	Gradient of QR	s	$f(s)$	Gradient of QS
2.9	2.159	8.41	3.1	3.961	9.61
the gradient at Q lies between 8.4 and 9.6					
2.99	2.9106	8.94	3.01	3.0906	9.06
the gradient at Q lies between 8.9 and 9.1					
2.999	2.991 006	8.994	3.001	3.009 006	9.006
the gradient at Q lies between 8.99 and 9.01					

To be more precise we can now see that the gradient at Q is more than 8.994, but less than 9.006. Therefore, it is almost certainly 9.00, correct to two decimal places. With the help of your calculator, you should be able to see that the next line would give limits of 8.9994 and 9.0006, to confirm this.

▷ **3** For the same function, find the coordinates of T, and the gradient at U, correct to two decimal places. (See Figure 1.) 11

▷ **4** Solve the equation $x - 3 + \frac{3}{x^2} = 0$ as follows.

(a) On the same axes sketch the graphs of $y = 3 - x$ and $y = \frac{3}{x^2}$ for $^{-}2 \leqslant x \leqslant 3$.

(b) Use your graph to find the approximate values of the x-coordinates of the points where the graphs cross.

(c) Use your calculator to find these values correct to two decimal places, and hence find the solutions of the original equation, correct to two decimal places.

5 (a) Sketch the graph of $y = x^3 - 80$ for $0 \leqslant x \leqslant 5$.

(b) Use your calculator to find the value of x (correct to three significant figures) between 0 and 5 for which $x^3 - 80 = 0$.

Hence write down the cube root of 80, correct to three significant figures. 12

Matrix multiplication

Calculators can be useful in finding the product of two matrices, particularly in transformation geometry.

Example 5. Find the image of the ship shown in Figure 3 under the transformation whose matrix is $\begin{bmatrix} 0.9 & 0.8 \\ 0.1 & 0.7 \end{bmatrix}$.

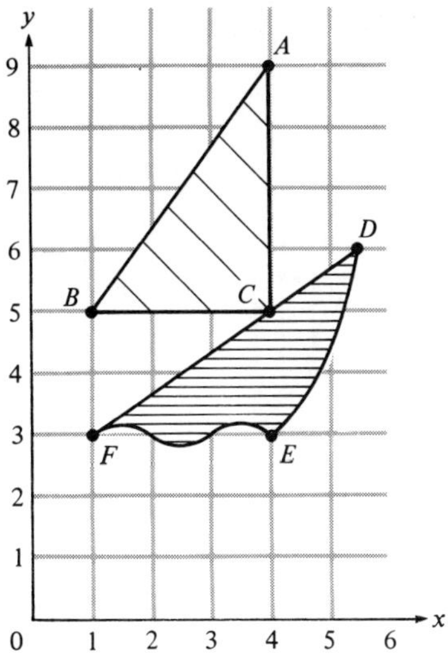

Figure 3

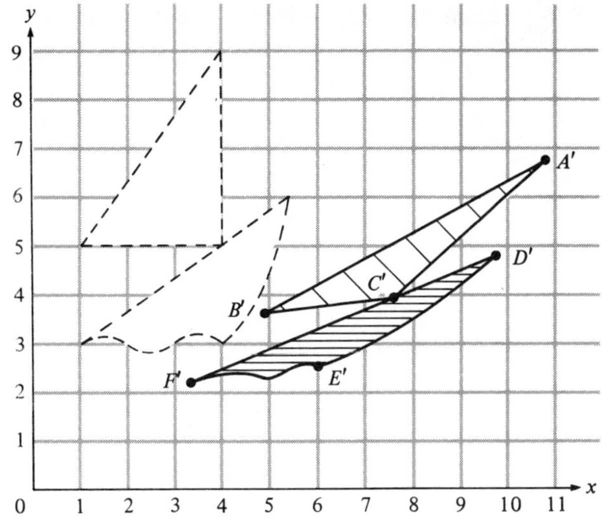

Figure 4

The coordinates of the images are found by the matrix multiplication

$$\begin{bmatrix} 0.9 & 0.8 \\ 0.1 & 0.7 \end{bmatrix} \begin{matrix} A & B & C & D & E & F \\ \left[\begin{matrix} 4 & 1 & 4 & 5.5 & 4 & 1 \\ 9 & 5 & 5 & 6 & 3 & 3 \end{matrix}\right] \end{matrix}.$$

(Remember that the *columns* of the second matrix contain the coordinates of the original points. To find, for example, the image of C, the x-coordinate is given by

$$[0.9 \quad 0.8] \begin{bmatrix} 4 \\ 5 \end{bmatrix} \text{, i.e. by } 0.9 \times 4 + 0.8 \times 5 \ (= 7.6),$$

and the y-coordinate by $[0.1 \quad 0.7] \begin{bmatrix} 4 \\ 5 \end{bmatrix}$ (= 3.9).

When using a calculator it is not necessary to write down these intermediate stages.)

The complete multiplication is

$$\begin{matrix} A' & B' & C' & D' & E' & F' \\ \left[\begin{matrix} 10.8 & 4.9 & 7.6 & 9.75 & 6.0 & 3.3 \\ 6.7 & 3.6 & 3.9 & 4.75 & 2.5 & 2.2 \end{matrix}\right] \end{matrix}.$$

Figure 4 shows the image superimposed on Figure 3.

▷ **6** (a) Make a copy of Figure 5, using a scale of 5 cm to 1 unit.

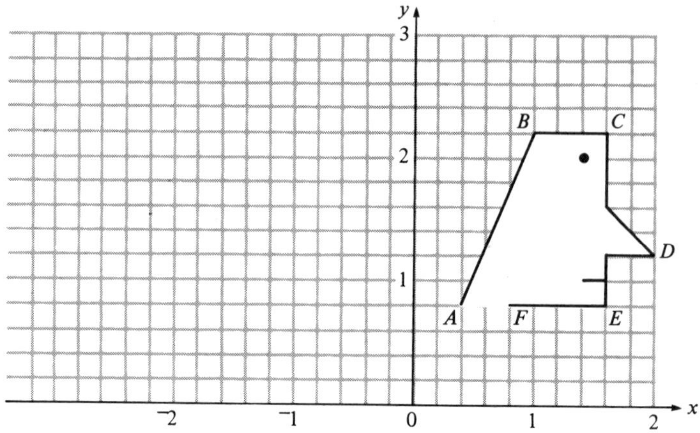

Figure 5

(b) Find the coordinates, correct to two decimal places, of the images of $A, B, C, D,$ E and F under the transformation **T** whose matrix is

$$\begin{bmatrix} \cos 120^\circ & {}^-\sin 120^\circ \\ \sin 120^\circ & \cos 120^\circ \end{bmatrix}.$$

(If your calculator does not have trigonometrical functions, use 0.8660 for sin 120° and ⁻0.5000 for cos 120°.)

(c) Draw the image of *ABCDEF* on your diagram, and describe the transformation **T** as fully as possible. 13

Exercise B

▷ **1** (a) The radius of a circle is quoted as 28 cm. Assuming this to be an 'exact' measurement, calculate the area of the circle using the following values for π.

22/7, 3.142, the [π] button (or 3.141 593)

(b) Using the third value of π quoted above, calculate the maximum and minimum area of the circle if the radius is correct only to the nearest centimetre.

2 (a) Draw the graph of $y = 5 - \dfrac{9.75}{x^2}$ for the following values of x.

1, 1.25, 1.5, 1.75, 2, 2.5, 3, 4, 5

(b) Find, correct to three significant figures, the gradient of this function at the point where it crosses the x-axis.

3 Make another copy of Figure 5 and find the image of *ABCDEF* under the transformation **U** whose matrix is $\begin{bmatrix} \cos 135^\circ & \sin 135^\circ \\ \sin 135^\circ & ^-\cos 135^\circ \end{bmatrix}$.
(If necessary, use 0.7071 for sin 135°, and ⁻0.7071 for cos 135°.)
Describe the transformation **U** as fully as possible. 14

2.3 Flow diagrams

Flow diagrams are used in numerical work when a complicated calculation needs to be broken up into smaller, more manageable, units; and when a sequence of operations has to be performed several times. As a simple example, when considering

$$f(x) = x^3 - 3x^2 + 3 = x^2(x - 3) + 3$$

in the last section it was helpful to have a routine such as

'square x, multiply by $(x - 3)$, add 3'

to evaluate $f(x)$ for a number of different values of x.

Earlier work with flow diagrams (see *Algebra 1: Language and Structure*) has been confined to situations in which the value of x is fed in once only (at the beginning of the calculation), as in questions 3 and 4 of the Pre-test. With such a flow diagram it is not necessary to use the memory of a calculator.

Many problems, however, require the value of x to be fed in more than once, and it becomes necessary to modify our 'rules' for flow diagrams. When a calculator is used, this involves storing the value of x in the memory, or re-entering it manually when it is needed again.

Another simplification in earlier work was that, as the diagram usually had only three or four boxes, it was possible to draw the diagram so that it 'flowed' across the page. For longer flow diagrams it is more convenient and useful to draw them to flow down the page. Figure 6 shows this for the function f: $x \rightarrow x^2(x - 3) + 3$.

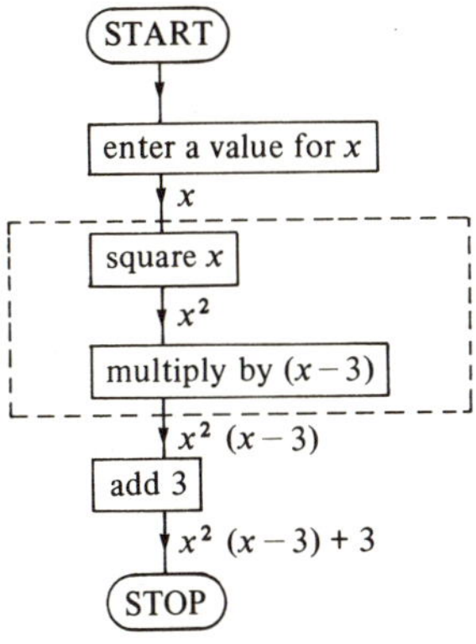

Figure 6

You should be able to use a flow diagram with any calculator or computer. In other words, it will tell you *what* has to be done, but it will not always tell you *how* to execute each stage.

Thus in Figure 6, the method used to carry out the two stages in the dotted area will vary from machine to machine. Some of the possible alternatives are listed below.

Alternative 1	*Alternative 2*†	*Alternative 3*
square x	subtract 3	store x in memory
call this result S	call this result T	square (x)
write down S*	write down T*	call this result S
re-enter the original value of x	add 3	exchange with memory#
subtract 3	square	subtract 3
multiply by S*	multiply by T*	multiply by S*

Notes: * If the calculator has a memory this step is replaced by 'store S (or T) in memory', and the last stage will involve the use of MR ('memory recall').

\# This puts x^2 into the memory and brings back x from the memory into the 'front line' of the calculator.

† Note how this alternative avoids the necessity of having to re-enter x manually. This avoids the possibility of miskeying at this stage.

▷ **1** (a) Use the flow diagram in Figure 7 to evaluate y, correct to four significant figures, for the following values of x.

2.5, 2.52, 2.528

(b) Write down the relation between y and x in the form $y = f(x)$. 15

With the modifications to our ideas about flow diagrams, it is possible to enter several variables into a flow diagram.

▷ **2** (a) Use the flow diagram in Figure 8 to evaluate A when $a = 50.0$, $b = 33.7$, and $c = 25.2$.

(b) What formula is illustrated by this flow diagram?

3 Draw the flow diagrams for questions 1 and 2 of Exercise B. 16

Loops

In question 1 above you were required to carry out the sequence three times, and you may have noticed that for the second and third calculations you started with the result of the previous sequence. (The figures may also remind you of Example 4!)

Such repetition, using the previous result, can be incorporated into a flow diagram using a loop. Figure 9(a) shows such a loop added to Figure 7, together with an instruction to *write down* the result at the end of each loop.

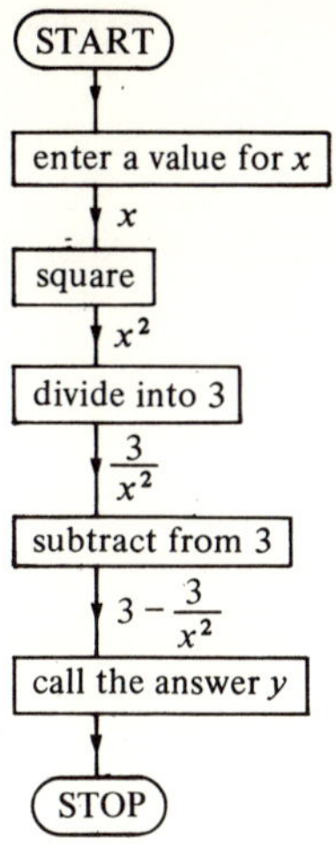

Figure 7

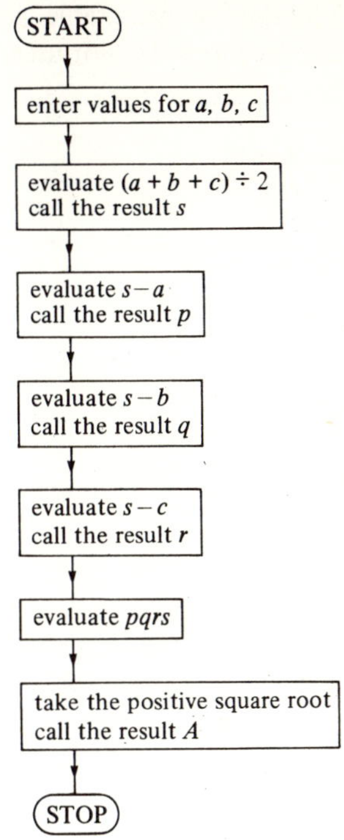

Figure 8

Check that you can obtain the following results (correct to four significant figures) by using the flow diagram in Figure 9(a).

	1st loop	2nd loop	3rd loop
x	2.500	(2.520)	(2.527 . . .)
Square	6.250	6.3504	6.389 . . .
Divide into 3	0.480	0.472. . .	0.470 . . .
Subtract from 3	2.520	2.527. . .	2.530 . . .
Write down	2.520	2.528	2.530

Note that, at the end of the second loop, we retained all the figures in the calculator, for use in the third loop.

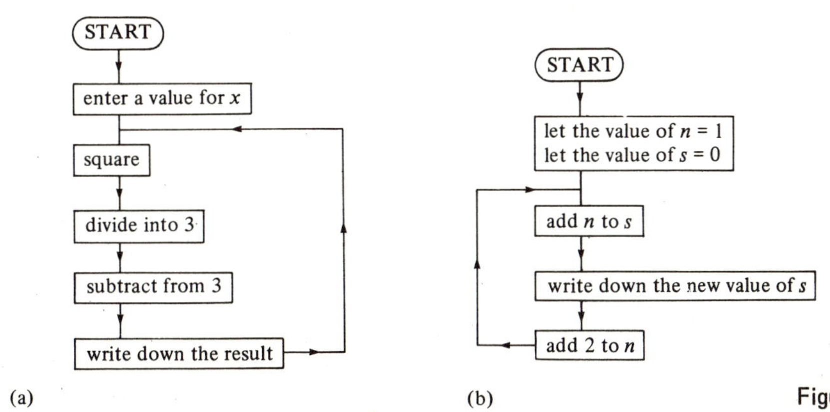

Figure 9

4 Copy the following table, and use the flow diagram in Figure 9(b) to complete the first five loops. Do not use a calculator!

Number of loop	1			2			3		4		5	
	n	s		n	s		n	s	n	s	n	s
Starting values	1	0	,	(3)	(1)	,	(5)	(4)				
Add n to s	1	1	,	3	4	,						
Write down s		1	,		4	,						
Add 2 to n	3	1	,	5	4	,						

What sequence of numbers is being generated by this flow diagram? 17

Decision boxes

One of the difficulties that arises when a loop is put into a flow diagram is that the process could now go on for ever! This is prevented by putting in a decision box to tell us (or the computer) when to stop. A decision box asks a question to which the answer is either YES or NO. This answer determines whether we return to the beginning – by travelling back along the loop – or not. A decision box is identified by being drawn as a diamond shape.

Figure 10 shows three possibilities for modifying Figure 9(b).

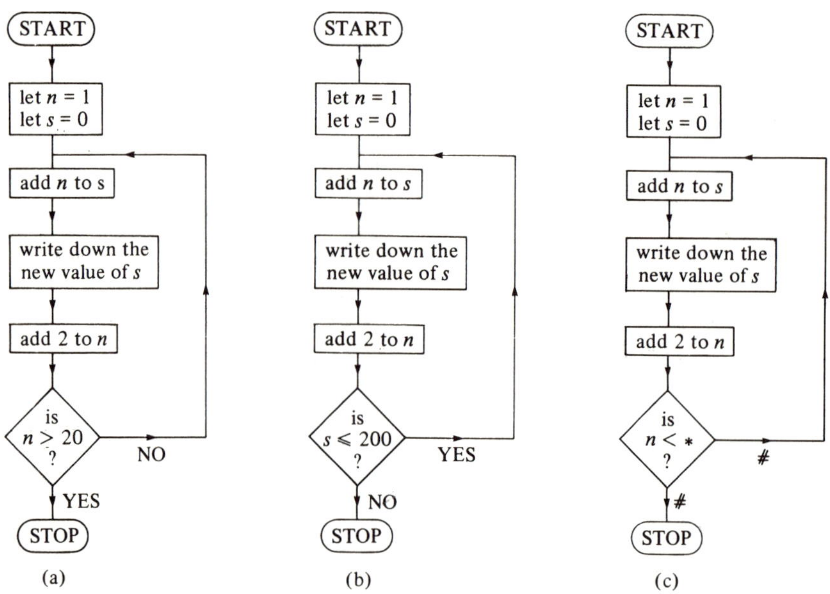

Figure 10

The flow diagram in Figure 10(a) tells us to stop after we have been round the loop ten times (i.e. after we have written down ten values for s). That in Figure 10(b) tells us to stop as soon as we have written down a value for s that is greater than 200.

5 (a) What number would you put in place of the '20' in the decision box in Figure 10(a) if you wanted to record a sequence of fifty numbers?

(b) What would you put in place of * and # in Figure 10(c) so that the calculations stop after recording fifteen values of s?

(c) Whereabouts in the flow diagram in Figure 10(b) could you put the decision box shown, so that the process stops as soon as you have written down the last number s that is not more than 200?

6 Redraw the flow diagram in Figure 6 so that it records the values of $f(x)$ for integral values of x from $^{-}3$ to $^{+}4$, inclusive. 18

For the flow diagram in Figure 9(a) we might want to stop the calculations when, to a given degree of accuracy, there is no change in the number being written down. A possible question would be

> 'Is the number now being written down the same, correct to four significant figures, as the last number that was written down?'

When the answer to this question is YES we stop, as we now have a result that is correct to four significant figures.

You may have found question 5(a) a little tricky. If a given number of results is required (ten say), it is sometimes easier to put in a separate 'counter'. This is labelled 'c' in Figure 11.

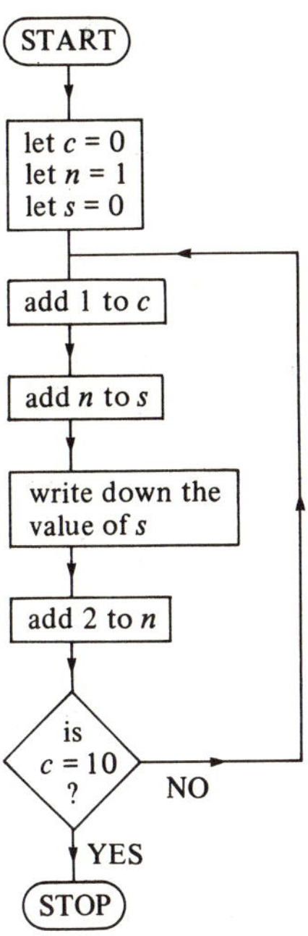

Figure 11

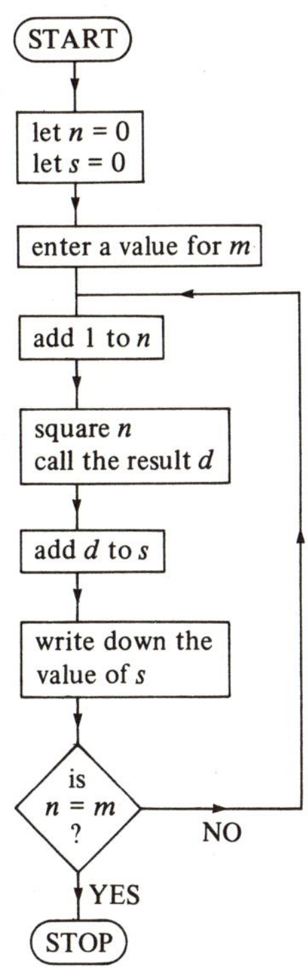

Figure 12

Exercise C

1 Figure 12 shows a flow diagram for calculating the first m pyramid numbers. (This flow diagram gives 'square-based' pyramid numbers.) Calculate the first eight members of this sequence.

2 Draw a flow diagram for calculating and recording the first twelve cube numbers. Use your calculator to find these numbers.

3 (a) From the flow diagram in Figure 13 calculate the values of p, q, r and s when $a = 8$, $b = c = 13$ and $d = 21$.
(b) Repeat part (a) when $a = 9, b = 16, c = 25$ and $d = 41$, giving the values of p, q, r and s correct to two decimal places.
(c) What operation is being carried out by this flow diagram?

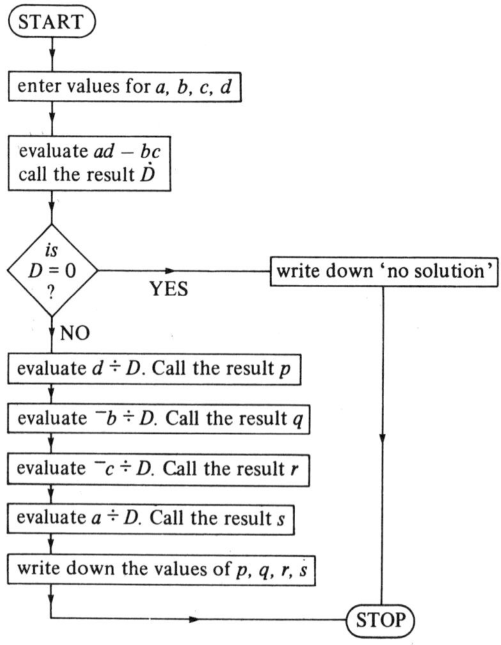

Figure 13 19

2.4 Iteration

Sequences

Figure 14 shows a flow diagram with a loop and a counter n. The table at the side of the diagram shows the stages as the first four loops are executed, starting with $x = 1$. (Results are entered correct to four decimal places.)

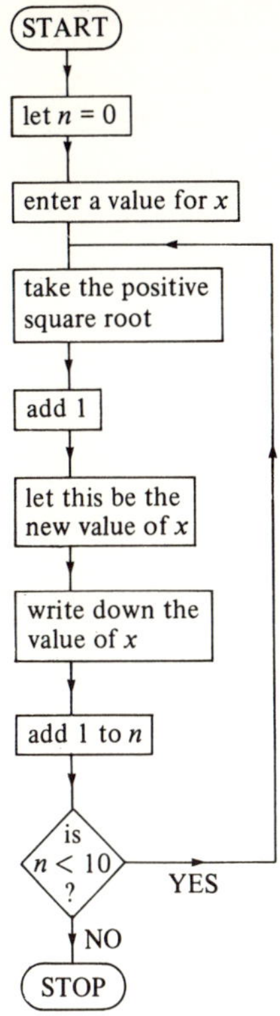

x	1	(2)	(2.4142)	(2.5538)
$\sqrt{x}$	1	1.4142	1.5538	1.5981
Add 1	2	2.4142	2.5538	2.5981
Write	2	2.4142	2.5538	2.5981
Add 1 to n	1	2	3	4
Is $n < 10$?	YES	YES	YES	YES

Figure 14

In this type of loop the result obtained at the end of the previous loop is used as the starting point for the new loop. The expression being evaluated in Figure 14 could therefore be written as

$$\text{new } x = \sqrt{(\text{old } x)} + 1.$$

A better way of distinguishing the various xs is as follows.

Let the first value of x to be used be x_0. (In this example $x_0 = 1$.)
Let the second value of x to be used be x_1.
(In this example $x_1 = \sqrt{x_0} + 1 = 2$.)
Let the third value of x to be used be x_2, and so on.
(In this example $x_2 = \sqrt{x_1} + 1 = 2.4142\ldots$,
$x_3 = \sqrt{x_2} + 1 = 2.5538\ldots$, and so on.)

Using the letter n to stand for any integer equal to or greater than 0, these results can all be written as

$$x_{n+1} = \sqrt{x_n} + 1,$$

i.e. instead of 'old x' we write 'x_n', and instead of 'new x' we write 'x_{n+1}'. If we are now given a starting value (in this example we started with $x_0 = 1$) we can use the flow diagram to evaluate $x_1, x_2, x_3, x_4, \ldots$ until the counter reaches the limit stated in the decision box. (If there is no decision box, the calculations can continue for as long as we please.)

This set of numbers $\left\{x_1,\ x_2,\ x_3,\ \ldots\right\}$ is sometimes called a *sequence*.

1 (a) Use your calculator to find $x_5, x_6, \ldots, x_{10}$ for the sequence started above.
(b) Execute the flow diagram in Figure 14 starting with $x_0 = 10$.

2 Find, correct to four significant figures, the first six terms of the sequence for which

$$x_{n+1} = \frac{1}{1 + x_n}$$

(a) starting with $x_0 = 1$,
(b) starting with $x_0 = 10$. 20

Limiting value

Sequences such as those described above are useful if they 'tend to a limit', i.e. if the values of successive xs are the same to a certain degree of accuracy. Thus in question 1 you showed that the sequence $x_{n+1} = \sqrt{x_n} + 1$ tends to a limit 2.618, correct to four significant figures.

3 State the limiting value, correct to two decimal places, of the sequence defined in question 2.

4 (a) Find the limiting value, correct to the nearest whole number, of the sequence $x_{n+1} = \sqrt{(x_n + 2)}$, starting with $x_0 = 1$.
(b) Find the limiting value, correct to the nearest whole number, of the sequence $x_{n+1} = \sqrt[3]{(x_n + 2)}$, starting with $x_0 = 1$.

5 Does the sequence $x_{n+1} = x_n^2 + 1$ have a limiting value? (Start with $x_0 = 1$; and then with $x_0 = 0.1$.) 21

Iterative solutions

In question 1 of Section 2.3 we obtained a sequence from the relation

$$x_{n+1} = 3 - (3/x_n^2),$$

and noted that the limit of this sequence appears to be a solution of the equation $x^3 - 3x^2 + 3 = 0$. (This process of repeating a routine is called *iteration*.)

This suggests the following method for finding one solution of an equation.

(1) Write the equation in the form $x = f(x)$.
(2) Find the sequence $\{x_n\}$ by iteration.
(3) If this sequence has a limiting value v, then $x = v$ is one solution of the original equation.

A solution to an equation found this way can be called an *iterative solution*.

Example 6. Find the solution between $x = 2$ and $x = 3$ of the equation $x^3 - 3x^2 + 3 = 0$ by an iterative method.
Start with the original equation $x^3 \quad 3x^2 + 3 = 0$.
Re-arrange so that there is just one term on the left-hand side. (This term must contain an x.)

For example, add $(3x^2 - 3)$ to both sides, giving $x^3 = 3x^2 - 3$.
Simplify the equation so that the left-hand side reads '$x =$ '.

For example, divide both sides by x^2, giving

$$x = \frac{3x^2 - 3}{x^2} = 3 - \frac{3}{x^2}.$$

We can now write down a relation

$$x_{n+1} = 3 - \frac{3}{x_n^2}.$$

Starting with $x_0 = 2.5$ this gives

$x_1 = 2.52$	$x_2 = 2.5276\ldots$	$x_3 = 2.5304\ldots$
$x_4 = 2.5315\ldots$	$x_5 = 2.5319\ldots$	$x_6 = 2.5320\ldots$
$x_7 = 2.5321\ldots$	$x_8 = 2.5321\ldots$	$x_9 = 2.5321\ldots$.

From this sequence we deduce that one solution of the original equation is $x = 2.532$, correct to four significant figures.

▷ **6** (a) Show that the equation $x^3 - 3x^2 + 3 = 0$ may be re-arranged as $x = \frac{x^2}{3} + \frac{1}{x}$.

(b) Starting with $x_0 = 1$, use the relation

$$x_{n+1} = \frac{x_n^2}{3} + \frac{1}{x_n}$$

to find another root, correct to three significant figures, of the equation $x^3 - 3x^2 + 3 = 0$. 22

▷ **7** (a) Show that the equation $x^2 - 2x - 5 = 0$ may be re-arranged as $x = 2 + \frac{5}{x}$.

(b) Find the limiting values, correct to two decimal places, of the sequence $x_{n+1} = 2 + \frac{5}{x_n}$ for the following values of x_0.

$^-4$, 10, 3, 3.5

(c) Verify that when $x = 3.45$, the value of $x^2 - 2x - 5$ is approximately zero.

(d) Sketch the graph of $y = x^2 - 2x - 5$ for $^-2 \leqslant x \leqslant {}^+4$, and use the symmetry of the parabola to state the other root of the equation $x^2 - 2x - 5 = 0$. 23

Iteration is a convenient method for finding some of the solutions of an equation. Question 7 above shows that even if x_0 is not very close to a root, the iteration often 'homes in' on a root very quickly – although it is not always the root nearest to x_0! If you are given the iteration, and a starting point (i.e. a value for x_0), the method is straightforward – but otherwise care is necessary, as not all the possible re-arrangements of an equation will give an iteration that has a limiting value.

Iteration is a useful method for cubic equations, and more difficult equations. It is not usually a recommended method for quadratic equations: quadratic equations are used in questions 7 and 8 above, and in Exercise D below, merely to give some fairly easy examples.

8 Two alternative re-arrangements of the equation in question 7 are $x = (x^2 - 5)/2$ and $x = \pm\sqrt{(2x + 5)}$.
Investigate the effect of using these relations iteratively with the following values for x_0.

$$4, \quad 3, \quad 0, \quad {}^{-}1, \quad {}^{-}2$$

24

Exercise D

In this exercise you are asked to attempt to solve the equation $100 + x - x^2 = 0$ by three iterative methods.

1 (a) Show that the equation may be written as $x = 1 + 100/x$.
(b) Use this relation to find an iterative solution (correct to one decimal place) starting with $x_0 = 10$.
(c) What happens if you use ${}^{-}10$ for x_0?

2 (a) Show that the equation may also be written as

$$x = \frac{100}{x - 1}.$$

(b) Use this relation to find an iterative solution, starting with $x_0 = {}^{-}10$.
(c) What happens if you start with $x_0 = 10$?

3 (a) Use the iteration $x = {}^{+}\sqrt{(x + 100)}$ with $x_0 = 10$; and with $x_0 = {}^{-}10$.
(b) Use the iteration $x = {}^{-}\sqrt{(x + 100)}$ with $x_0 = 10$; and with $x_0 = {}^{-}10$.

4 Verify that the two different values that you have obtained are both approximate solutions of the equation $100 + x - x^2 = 0$.

25

Summary

(1) When using a calculator to evaluate a numerical problem
(a) write down on paper the calculation that you are going to do;
(b) consider the most effective order of performing the various stages of the calculation;
(c) work to the full capacity of the machine;
(d) check your answer both mentally (does it look right?) and by performing the calculation again in a different order;
(e) give answers to a suitable and sensible degree of accuracy.

(2) Section 2.2 illustrates the use of a calculator in problems involving matrices, graphs, and limits of accuracy.

(3) A flow diagram is a diagrammatic representation of the various stages in a complex calculation. The diagram shows what stages have to be performed; it does not necessarily explain in detail how to do each stage.

If a sequence of operations is to be performed several times, a loop is introduced into the flow diagram. In such cases, the number on the calculator is written down at the end of each loop. This set of numbers is sometimes described as a sequence.

If a flow diagram contains a loop, then it usually has a decision box as well, to indicate when to stop going round the loop.

(4) In the iterative method for solving equations, the original equation $f(x) = 0$ is rewritten in a form $x = F(x)$. The relation $x_{n+1} = F(x_n)$ is then used with a given value of x_0 to evaluate x_n for successive values of n. If this sequence tends to a limiting value, then this value is one of the solutions of the original equation.

Post-test

▷ 1 The table below is a summary of the yields of 58 tomato plants. Copy and complete the table, and calculate the mean average yield per plant, correct to three significant figures.

Yield	Frequency (f)	Mid-point of yield (x)	$f \times x$
less than 1 kg	2	0.50 kg	1.00
1.00–1.99 kg	5	1.50 kg	7.50
2.00–2.99 kg	13		
3.00–3.99 kg	21		
4.00–4.99 kg	16		
5.00–5.99 kg	1		
totals	58 plants	–	kg

Mean average yield = kg/plant.

2 Figure 15(a) shows part of a regular polygon with n sides, inscribed in a circle of radius r cm. Figure 15(b) is a flow diagram for calculating the perimeter, p cm, of the polygon for successive values of n. (See page 48.)

Starting with $n = 5$, calculate values of p (correct to two decimal places) when $r = 5$ and $m = 10$.

3 The equation $x^3 - x - 10 = 0$ may be written as

(a) $x = {}^{+}\sqrt{(1 + 10/x)}$ or (b) $x = \dfrac{10}{x^2 - 1}$.

Investigate the iterative solutions (correct to two decimal places) obtained from these relations for the following values of x_0.

0, 2, 3, 10

26 ▶

Assignment

1 When expressed as a decimal, the fraction $\frac{1}{17}$ recurs after the sixteenth decimal place.

(a) Evaluate 1/17, 2/17, 3/17, 4/17 and 5/17, correct to six decimal places, and hence 'piece together' the recurring decimal for 1/17.

(b) From this result write down, without further calculation, the recurring decimals for 10/17 and 11/17.

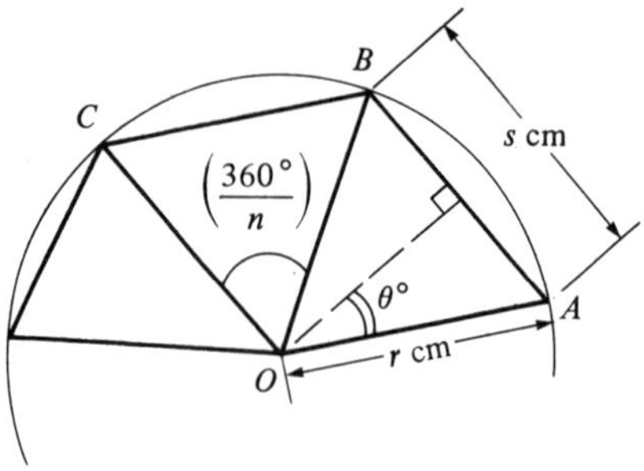

(a)

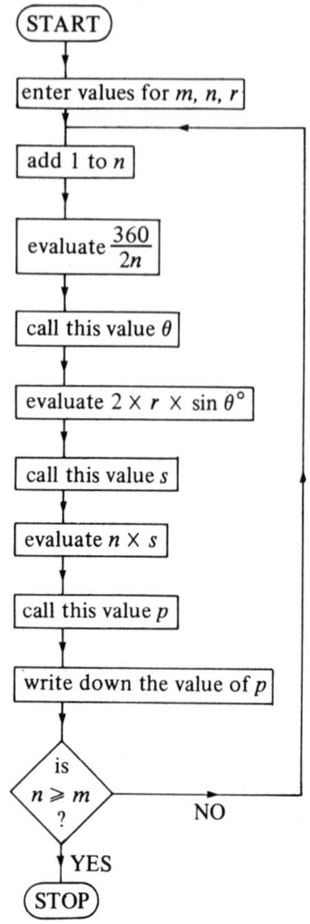

(b)

Figure 15

2 $f: x \to x^3 - 5x - 1$

(a) Draw a flow diagram for evaluating $f(x)$ for integral values of x from $^-3$ to 3 inclusive.

(b) Draw the graph of this function for $^-3 \leqslant x \leqslant 3$, and hence estimate the roots of the equation $f(x) = 0$, correct to one decimal place.

(c) The equation may be written in the form $x = F(x)$, where F may be any one of the following.

$$(x^3 - 1)/5, \quad 1/(x^2 - 5), \quad {}^+\sqrt{(5 + 1/x)}, \quad {}^-\sqrt{(5 + 1/x)}$$

Investigate the effect of using each of these forms for solving the equation $f(x) = 0$ by iteration.
(Use the graph drawn for part (b) as a guide for values of x_0.)

Answers

Pre-test

▶1 1 (a) 43 (b) 99 (c) 37 (d) 91 (e) 14
(f) 8 (g) 5 (h) 2 (i) 28 (j) 64
(k) $^{-}9$ (l) 5 (m) $^{-}14$ (n) $^{+}14$ (o) 29
(p) $^{-}21$ (q) 1 (r) 9 (s) 4 (t) 1

2 Volume = $\frac{4}{\cancel{3}} \times \frac{22}{\cancel{7}} \times \cancel{21} \times 21 \times 21\ \text{cm}^3 = 88 \times 441\ \text{cm}^3 = 38\,808\ \text{cm}^3$.

3 (a) 4 ➤ 16 ➤ 48 ➤ 49 ➤ 7 ➤ $y = 7$.

(b) $y = \sqrt{(3x^2 + 1)}$

4

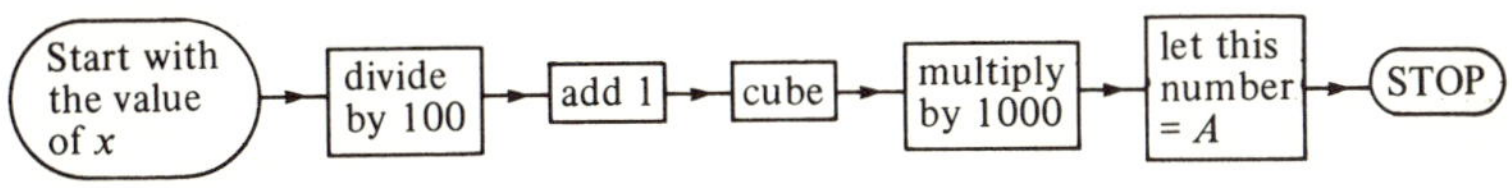

When $x = 20$, $A = 1728$.

2.1 Using a calculator

▶2 1 Some care may be needed with parts (k) to (p) that contain negative numbers.

2 (a) 38 808 cm^3 (b) 38 797 cm^3 (c) 38 792 cm^3

In parts (b) and (c) the answers are given correct to the nearest whole number. Notice from these results that the answer using 22/7 for π is correct only to three significant figures, i.e. the answer using 22/7 should be given as 38 800 cm^3 (to 3 s.f.).

▶3 3 (a) 12 (b) 3.794 733 2 (c) 1.2 (d) 0.379 473 3 (e) 0.12
(f) A negative number does not have a (real) square root, therefore your calculator should indicate error in some way – e.g. 'error', or 'E', or a string of 9s – if it doesn't, beware!

▶4 4 The exact answer is 974 192 654 016. For the calculator display see the text following the question.

▶5 5 (a) 5.6088 (b) 5.6088×10^{39}
(c) From the previous two answers it should be obvious that the answer is 5.6088×10^{156} (but as this number is too large for nearly all calculators you will probably get an 'overflow' or 'error' result).

▶6 6 For example:

1.449 93 → [÷ 4.31] → [× 11.46] → 3.855 266

1.416 88 → [× 11.46] → [÷ 4.31] → 3.767 389

The correct answer is 1.410 340 3 . . . .
The 'answer' 14.4993 was obtained by keying in 44.31 instead of 4.31, and the 'answer' 1.416 88 was obtained by keying in 4.33 instead of 4.31 – two examples of miskeying that might occur.

7 7 $3.409\,279 \times 10^{68}$.

8 8 Volume of 'bobbing dunce' $= \dfrac{\pi r^2(2r+h)}{3}$

$= \dfrac{\pi \times (4.2)^2 \times (2 \times 4.2 + 5.6)}{3}\ \text{cm}^3$

$= 258.6159\ldots\ \text{cm}^3$ (by calculator)

$= 259\ \text{cm}^3$ (correct to 3 s.f.).

Exercise A

9 1 (a) 100.25 (b) $0.035\,106\,6\ldots$

2 Total surface area $= \pi r(r+s)$ where $s^2 = r^2 + h^2 = (7.5)^2 + (16.3)^2 = 321.94$

$= \pi \times 7.5 \times (7.5 + 17.942\,687\ldots)\ \text{cm}^2$

$= 599.479\,18\ldots\ \text{cm}^2$ (by calculator)

$= 599\ \text{cm}^2$ (to 3 s.f.).

3 Calculate s first. $s = \frac{1}{2}(a+b+c)$

$= \frac{1}{2}(8.3 + 5.7 + 12.1)$ (cm)

$= 13.05$ (cm).

Hence the area of the triangle

$= \sqrt{[13.05 \times (13.05 - 8.3) \times (13.05 - 5.7) \times (13.05 - 12.1)]}\ \text{cm}^2$

$= \sqrt{(13.05 \times 4.75 \times 7.35 \times 0.95)}\ \text{cm}^2$

$= 20.804\,512\ \text{cm}^2$ (by calculator)

$= 20.8\ \text{cm}^2$ (correct to 3 s.f.).

2.2 Some applications

10 1 (a) Volume $= 20\ \text{cm} \times 7\ \text{cm} \times 29\ \text{cm} = 4060\ \text{cm}^3$.

(b) Maximum possible volume $= 20.5\ \text{cm} \times 7.5\ \text{cm} \times 29.5\ \text{cm}$

$= 4535.625\ \text{cm}^3$;

minimum possible volume $= 19.5\ \text{cm} \times 6.5\ \text{cm} \times 28.5\ \text{cm}$

$= 3612.375\ \text{cm}^3$.

If the measurements are correct only to the nearest centimetre (i.e. correct to two significant figures, more or less), then the volume should be quoted as

$4000\ \text{cm}^3$, correct to one significant figure.

2 (a) Maximum possible volume $= 20.1\ \text{cm} \times 7.1\ \text{cm} \times 29.1\ \text{cm}$

$= 4152.861\ \text{cm}^3$;

minimum possible volume $= 19.9\ \text{cm} \times 6.9\ \text{cm} \times 28.9\ \text{cm}$

$= 3968.259\ \text{cm}^3$.

It is still not possible to give an answer correct to two significant figures with any certainty. Some possible ways of expressing the answer are:

$4000\ \text{cm}^3$ or $4100\ \text{cm}^3$, correct to two significant figures;
$4100\ (\pm 100)\ \text{cm}^3$, correct to two significant figures;
$4060 \pm 100\ \text{cm}^3$.
(This implies that the exact volume is between $3960\ \text{cm}^3$ and $4160\ \text{cm}^3$.)

(b) Maximum possible volume = 20.05 cm x 7.05 cm x 29.05 cm
= 4106.290 cm^3;
minimum possible volume = 19.95 cm x 6.95 cm x 28.95 cm
= 4013.990 cm^3.

The volume is 4000 cm^3 or 4100 cm^3, correct to 2 s.f.; or the volume is 4060 ± 50 cm^3.

11 3 From the graph, the x-coordinate of T is about 1.4.

x	1.3	1.4
$f(x)$	0.127	⁻0.136

x	1.33	1.34	1.35
$f(x)$	0.046	0.019	⁻0.007

The coordinates of T are (1.35, 0), correct to 2 d.p.
The coordinates of U are (1, 1).
If V is the point $(v, f(v))$, then the gradient of UV is

$$\frac{f(v)-1}{v-1}.$$

v	$f(v)$	Gradient of UV
0.9	1.299	⁻2.99
0.99	1.029 999	⁻2.9999

v'	$f(v')$	Gradient of UV'
1.1	0.701	⁻2.99
1.01	0.970 001	⁻2.9999

The gradient at U is ⁻3.00, correct to two decimal places.
(Notice that U is a 'point of inflexion'; i.e. the gradient at U is steeper than at points either side of U. See Figure A.)

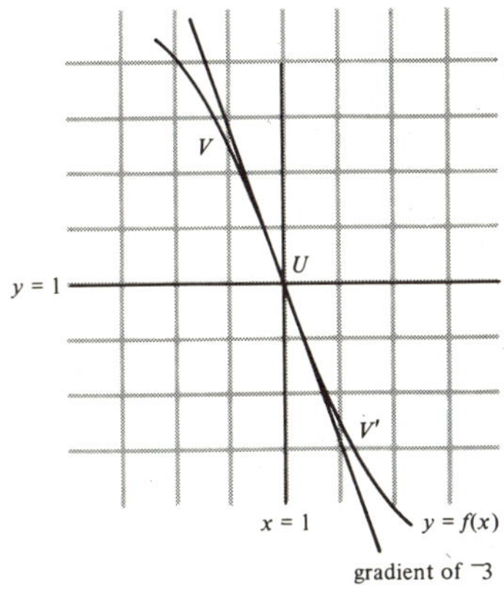

Figure A

12 **4** (a) See Figure B.

x	$^{-}2$	$^{-}1$	0	1	2	3
$3-x$	5	4	3	2	1	0
$3/x^2$	0.75	3	–	3	0.75	0.33

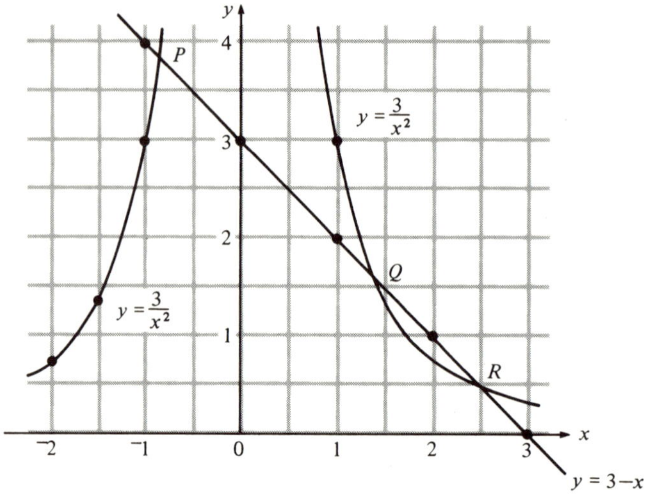

Figure B

(b)

Point	P	Q	R
x-coordinate	$^{-}0.8$	1.3	2.5

(c) Point P

x	$^{-}0.9$	$^{-}0.8$	$^{-}0.89$	$^{-}0.88$	$^{-}0.87$
$3-x$	3.9	3.8	3.89	3.88	3.87
$3/x^2$	3.704	4.688	3.787	3.874	3.964

Point Q

x	1.2	1.3	1.4	1.34	1.35	1.36
$3-x$	1.8	1.7	1.6	1.66	1.65	1.64
$3/x^2$	2.083	1.775	1.531	1.671	1.646	1.622

Point R

x	2.4	2.5	2.6	2.51	2.52	2.53	2.54
$3-x$	0.6	0.5	0.4	0.49	0.48	0.47	0.46
$3/x^2$	0.521	0.480	0.444	0.476	0.472	0.469	0.465

The x-coordinates, correct to two decimal places, and hence the solutions of the equation, correct to two decimal places, are

P	Q	R
$^{-}0.88$	1.35	2.53

Figure C illustrates the figures above for the point Q.
(Note that the equation in this question is really the same equation as in Example 4.)

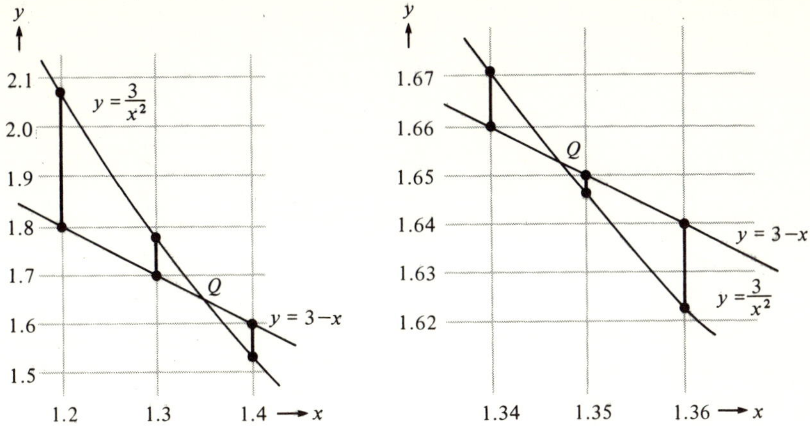

(a) (b)

Figure C

5 (a) See Figure D.

x	0	1	2	3	4	5
y	$^{-}80$	$^{-}79$	$^{-}72$	$^{-}53$	$^{-}16$	45

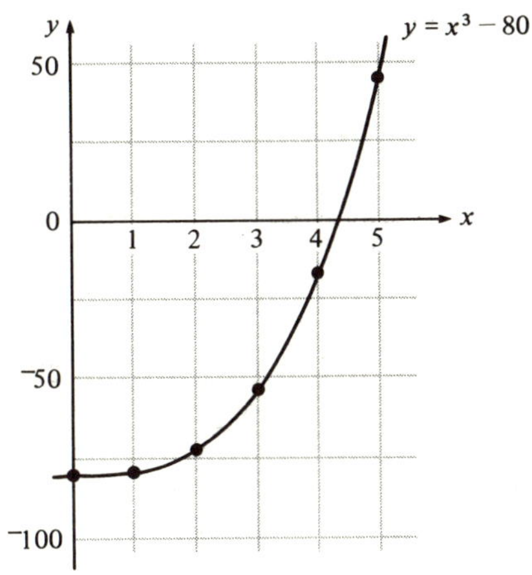

Figure D

(b) From the graph, the curve crosses the x-axis ($y = 0$) at about $x = 4.3$.

x	4.2	4.3
$x^3 - 80$	$^{-}5.912$	$^{-}0.493$

4.30	4.31	4.32
$^{-}0.493$	0.062...	0.622...

Therefore $x^3 - 80 = 0$ for $x = 4.31$, correct to 3 s.f.
The cube root of 80 is 4.31, correct to 3 s.f.

13 **6** (a) See Figure E.

(b)

$$\begin{bmatrix} \cos 120° & {}^{-}\sin 120° \\ \sin 120° & \cos 120° \end{bmatrix} \begin{matrix} A & B & C & D & E & F \\ \left[\begin{matrix} 0.4 & 1.0 & 1.6 & 2.0 & 1.6 & 0.8 \\ 0.8 & 2.2 & 2.2 & 1.2 & 0.8 & 0.8 \end{matrix}\right] \end{matrix}$$

$$= \begin{matrix} A' & B' & C' & D' & E' & F' \\ \left[\begin{matrix} {}^{-}0.892 & {}^{-}2.405 & {}^{-}2.705 & {}^{-}2.039 & {}^{-}1.493 & {}^{-}1.093 \\ {}^{-}0.054 & {}^{-}0.234 & 0.286 & 1.132 & 0.986 & 0.293 \end{matrix}\right] \end{matrix}$$

(All figures are given to three decimal places only.)

(c) See Figure E.
The transformation is a rotation about the origin through an angle of 120° (anti-clockwise).

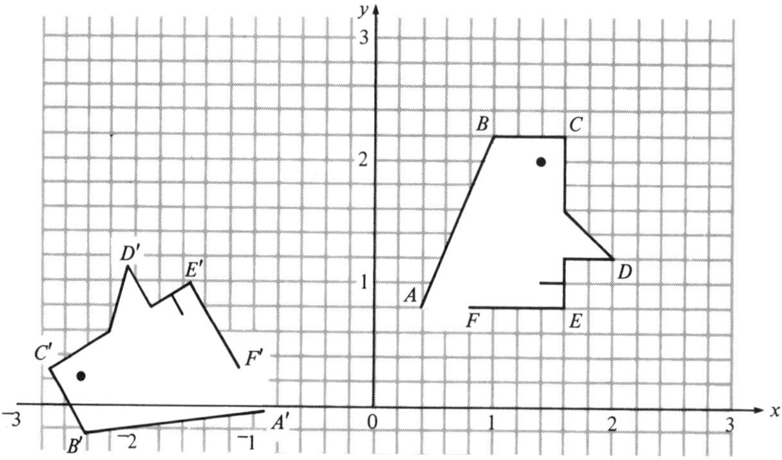

Figure E

Exercise B

14 **1** (a) Area = πr^2. 2464 cm², 2463.328 cm², 2463.009 . . . cm².
(The value 22/7 for π gives an answer correct to three significant figures.)

(b) Maximum possible area = $\pi \times (28.5)^2$ cm² = 2551.759 . . . cm²;
minimum possible area = $\pi \times (27.5)^2$ cm² = 2375.829 . . . cm².
Hence if the radius is correct only to the nearest centimetre, the area of the circle should be quoted as 2400 cm² or 2500 cm², correct to two significant figures; or as 2460 ± 100 cm².

2 (a) See Figure F.

x	1	1.25	1.5	1.75	2	2.5	3	4	5
y	⁻4.75	⁻1.24	0.67	1.82	2.56	3.44	3.92	4.39	4.61

(The values of y are given correct to two decimal places.)

(b) Let the point where the curve crosses the x-axis be G.
From the graph, the x-coordinate of G is approximately 1.4.

x	1.35	1.40	1.38	1.39	1.40
y	$^-0.350$	0.026	$^-0.119\,723$	$^-0.046\,323$	0.025 510

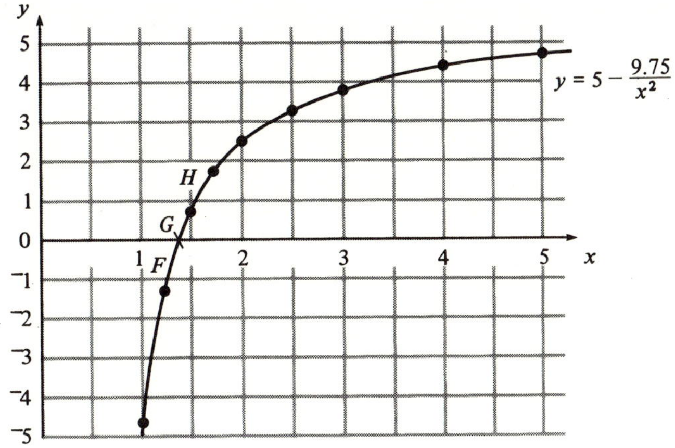

Figure F

Hence the x-coordinate of G is 1.40, correct to three significant figures.
Looking at the values of y for $x = 1.39$ and $x = 1.40$ suggests that a more accurate value for the x-coordinate of G would be 1.396 or 1.397.

x	1.396	1.397
y	$^-0.003\,038$	0.004 122

Let the points with these x-coordinates be F and H.
As F and H are either side of G, but very close to G, the gradient of the chord FH will be very nearly the same as the gradient at G.

$$\text{Hence gradient at } G \text{ is approximately } \frac{0.004\,122 - (^-0.003\,038)}{1.397 - 1.396} = 7.160\ldots$$

$$= 7.16 \text{ (to 3 s.f.).}$$

3

$$\begin{bmatrix} \cos 135^\circ & \sin 135^\circ \\ \sin 135^\circ & ^-\cos 135^\circ \end{bmatrix} \begin{bmatrix} \overset{A}{0.4} & \overset{B}{1.0} & \overset{C}{1.6} & \overset{D}{2.0} & \overset{E}{1.6} & \overset{F}{0.8} \\ 0.8 & 2.2 & 2.2 & 1.2 & 0.8 & 0.8 \end{bmatrix}$$

$$= \begin{bmatrix} \overset{A'}{0.283} & \overset{B'}{0.849} & \overset{C'}{0.424} & \overset{D'}{^-0.566} & \overset{E'}{^-0.566} & \overset{F'}{0} \\ 0.849 & 2.263 & 2.687 & 2.263 & 1.697 & 1.131 \end{bmatrix}$$

See Figure G. The transformation is a reflection in the line OZ, where OZ makes an angle of $67\frac{1}{2}^\circ$ (half of 135°) with the x-axis.

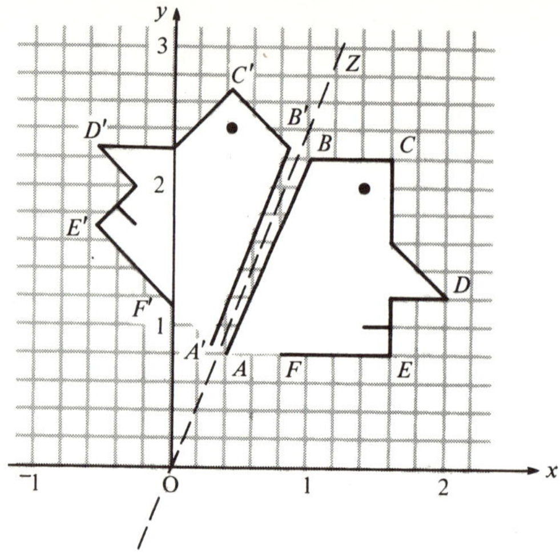

Figure G

2.3 Flow diagrams

15 **1** (a) 2.520, 2.528, 2.530 (All results are correct to four significant figures.)

(b) $y = 3 - \dfrac{3}{x^2}$

16 **2** (a) $s = 54.45$, $p = 4.45$, $q = 20.75$, $r = 29.25$, $A = 383.5$ (correct to four significant figures).

(b) $A = \sqrt{[s(s-a)(s-b)(s-c)]}$ for working out the area of a triangle whose sides are of lengths a, b and c.

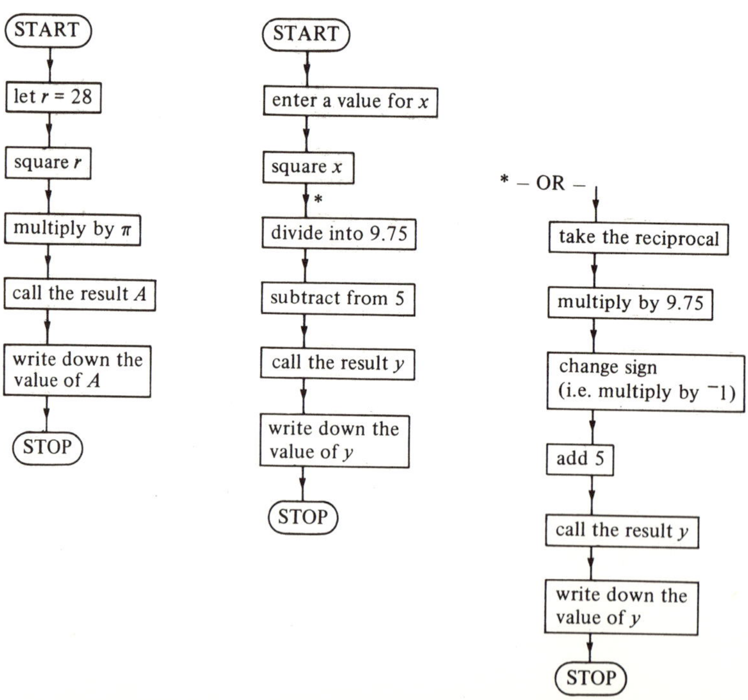

Figure H

3 See Figure H which shows detailed flow diagrams.
(Your answer may have combined some of the stages.)

Note how the alternative flow diagram in Figure H(b) uses the *reciprocal* ($1/x$) and *change sign* keys to overcome the difficulties caused by *divide into* . . . and *subtract from* . . . .

17 4

Number of loop	1		2		3		4		5	
	n	s	n	s	n	s	n	s	n	s
Starting values	1	0	(3)	(1)	(5)	(4)	(7)	(9)	(9)	(16)
Add n to s	1	1	3	4	5	9	7	16	9	25
Write down s		1		4		9		16		25
Add 2 to n	3	1	5	4	7	9	9	16	11	25

The numbers written down (the numbers underlined in the table above) are the *square numbers*.

18 5 (a) 100
(b) For * put 30, and for # put YES to return round the loop, and NO to proceed to STOP.
(c) See Figure I.

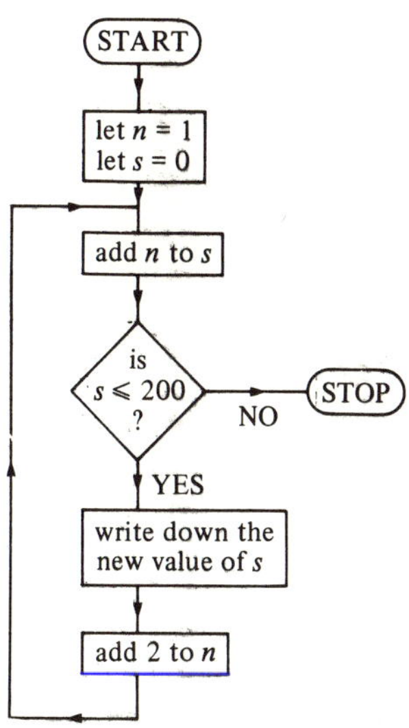

Figure I

6 See Figure J.

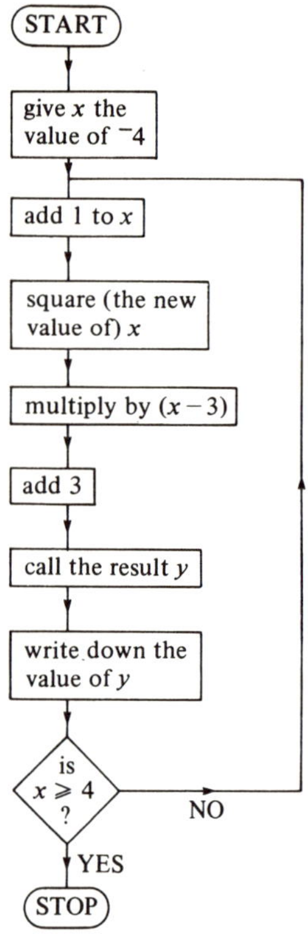

Figure J

Exercise C

19 **1** To record eight values, m must be given the value 8.

n	1	2	3	4	5	6	7	8
d	1	4	9	16	25	36	49	64
s	<u>1</u>	<u>5</u>	<u>14</u>	<u>30</u>	<u>55</u>	<u>91</u>	<u>140</u>	<u>204</u>

n is now equal to m (8), so we STOP.

The eight values of s are the first eight pyramid numbers.

2 See Figure K.
1, 8, 27, 64, 125, 216, 343, 512, 729, 1000, 1331, 1728

3 (a) $D = {}^-1$, $p = {}^-21$, $q = 13$, $r = 13$, $s = {}^-8$
(b) $D = {}^-31$, $p = {}^-1.32$, $q = 0.52$, $r = 0.81$, $s = {}^-0.29$
(The last four results are correct to two decimal places.)
(c) For the matrix $\begin{bmatrix} a & b \\ c & d \end{bmatrix}$, D is the value of the determinant, and the inverse matrix is $\begin{bmatrix} p & q \\ r & s \end{bmatrix}$. If $D = 0$, then there is no inverse.

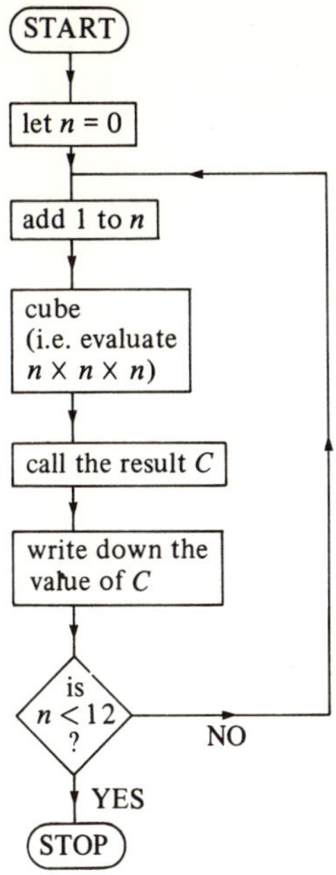

Figure K

2.4 Iteration

20 **1** (a) $x_5 = 2.6118\ldots$ $x_6 = 2.6161\ldots$ $x_7 = 2.6174\ldots$
$x_8 = 2.6179\ldots$ $x_9 = 2.6180\ldots$ $x_{10} = 2.6180\ldots$

(b) $x_0 = 10$ $x_1 = 4.1623\ldots$ $x_2 = 3.0402\ldots$ $x_3 = 2.7436\ldots$
$x_4 = 2.6564\ldots$ $x_5 = 2.6298\ldots$ $x_6 = 2.6217\ldots$ $x_7 = 2.6192\ldots$
$x_8 = 2.6184\ldots$ $x_9 = 2.6181\ldots$ $x_{10} = 2.6181\ldots$

2

	x_0	x_1	x_2	x_3	x_4	x_5	x_6
(a)	1	0.5	0.6666...	0.6	0.625	0.6154...	0.6190...
(b)	10	0.0909...	0.9167...	0.5217...	0.6571...	0.6034...	0.6237...

21 **3** 0.62

4

	x_0	x_1	x_2	x_3	x_4	x_5	x_6
(a)	1	1.7321..	1.9319..	1.9829..	1.9957..	1.9989..	1.9997..
(b)	1	$^-$1.7321..	$^-$0.5176..	$^-$1.2175..	$^-$0.8846..	$^-$1.0561..	$^-$0.9715..

The limiting value for (a) is 2, and for (b) is $^-1$.

5 1, 2, 5, 26, 677, ...
0.1, 1.01..., 2.02..., 5.08..., 26.8..., ...
This sequence does not have a limiting value.

22 **6** (a) $x^3 - 3x^2 + 3 = 0$ can be re-arranged as $3x^2 = x^3 + 3$.

Dividing both sides by $3x$ gives $$x = \frac{x^2}{3} + \frac{1}{x}.$$

(b) The sequence is ($x_0 = 1$), 1.333..., 1.342..., 1.345..., 1.346..., 1.347..., 1.347..., ...
Another root, correct to three significant figures, is $x = 1.35$.

23 **7** (a) $x^2 - 2x - 5 = 0$ may be re-arranged as $x^2 = 2x + 5$.

Dividing both sides by x gives $$x = 2 + \frac{5}{x}.$$

(b) For each value of x_0, the limiting value of the sequence, correct to two decimal places, is 3.45.

(c) If $x^2 - 5x - 5$ is written as $f(x)$, then $f(3.45) = 11.9025 - 6.90 - 5 = 0.0025$.

(d) See Figure L.

x	$^-2$	$^-1$	0	1	2	3	4
y	3	$^-2$	$^-5$	$^-6$	$^-5$	$^-2$	3

The line of symmetry is $x = 1$, and so the other solution is $1 - 2.45 = {}^-1.45$, correct to two decimal places.

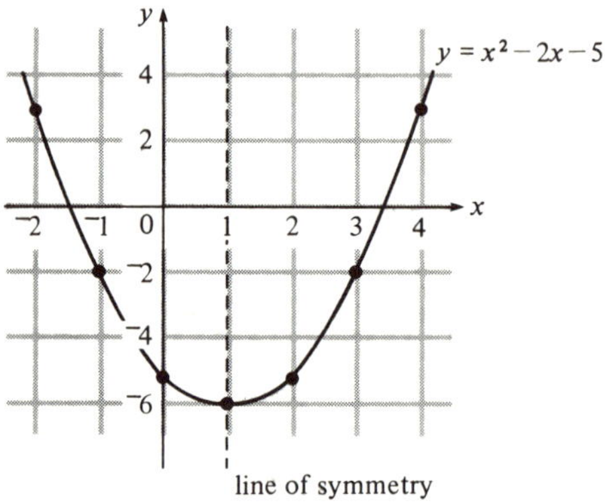

Figure L

24 **8** The sequence $x_{n+1} = (x_n^2 - 5)/2$ does not have a limiting value for any value of x_0.
The sequence $x_{n+1} = {}^+\sqrt{(2x_n + 5)}$ has a limiting value of 3.45 (correct to two decimal places) for all the values of x_0.
The sequence $x_{n+1} = {}^-\sqrt{(2x_n + 5)}$ has no limiting value for $x_0 = 4$ or $x_0 = 3$; but for $x_0 = 0, {}^-1$, and $^-2$ the limiting value is $^-1.45$ (correct to two decimal places).
(As it is not possible to have a real square root of a negative number, the sequence breaks down as soon as $2x + 5 < 0$; to obtain a limiting value $^-2.5 \leqslant x_0 \leqslant 0.625$.)

Exercise D

25 **1** (a) $100 + x - x^2 = 0$ may be re-arranged as $x^2 = x + 100$.

Dividing both sides by x gives $$x = 1 + \frac{100}{x}.$$

(b) $x_0 = 10$ gives 11, 10.09 . . . , 10.90 . . . , ...
This sequence slowly approaches a limit 10.51 . . . , or 10.5 correct to one decimal place.

(c) Starting with $x_0 = {}^-10$, the sequence does not approach a limiting value.

2 (a) Re-arranging the equation as $x^2 - x = 100$,
factorising the left-hand side; $x(x - 1) = 100$,
and dividing both sides by $(x - 1)$; $x = \dfrac{100}{x - 1}$.

(b) $x_0 = {}^-10$ gives $^-9.09\ldots$, $^-9.90\ldots$, ...
This sequence slowly approaches a limiting value of $^-9.51\ldots$, or $^-9.5$ correct to one decimal place.

(c) Starting with $x_0 = 10$, the sequence does not approach a limiting value.

3 (a) $x_0 = 10$ gives 10.48..., 10.51..., 10.51..., ...
Notice how this iteration very quickly gives a limiting value of 10.5125....
$x_0 = {}^-10$ also gives this limiting value very quickly.

(b) Both values of x_0 quickly give a limiting value of $^-9.5125\ldots$.

4 If $100 + x - x^2$ is written as $f(x)$, then

$$f(10.5) = 100 + 10.5 - 110.25 = 0.25,$$
$$f(10.51) = 100 + 10.51 - 110.4601 = 0.0499,$$
$$f(10.5125) = 100 + 10.5125 - 110.5127\ldots = {}^-0.0002\ldots,$$
$$f({}^-9.5) = 0.25, \quad f({}^-9.51) = 0.0499\ldots,$$
$$f({}^-9.5125) = {}^-0.0002\ldots.$$

Post-test

26 1

Yield	Frequency (f)	Mid-point of yield (x)	$f \times x$
less than 1 kg	2	0.50 kg	1.00
1.00–1.99 kg	5	1.50 kg	7.50
2.00–2.99 kg	13	2.50 kg	32.50
3.00–3.99 kg	21	3.50 kg	73.50
4.00–4.99 kg	16	4.50 kg	72.00
5.00–5.99 kg	1	5.50 kg	5.50
Totals	58 plants	–	192.00 kg

Mean average yield $= \dfrac{192}{58}$ kg/plant
= 3.3103... kg/plant,
= 3.31 kg/plant (to 3 s.f.).

2

n	5	(6)	(7)	(8)	(9)	
Add 1 to n	6	7	8	9	10	
$\theta = \dfrac{360}{2n}$	30	25.714...	22.5	20	18	
$s = 2r \sin \theta°$	5	4.338...	3.826...	3.420...	3.090...	$(r = 5)$
$p = ns$	30	30.371...	30.614...	30.781...	30.901...	
Write p	30	30.37	30.61	30.78	30.90	
Is $n \geqslant m$?	NO	NO	NO	NO	YES → STOP	$(m = 10)$

As the number of sides increases, the length of the perimeter becomes closer to the circumference of the circle. Archimedes used this method as an estimate for the value of π, by dividing the perimeter by the diameter. (He found the length of s by applying Pythagoras' theorem.)

3 (a) $x_0 = 0$ is not possible. (It is not possible to divide by 0.) The other values for x_0 all lead to a limiting value of 2.3089..., = 2.31, correct to two decimal places.

(b) The second relation does not have a limiting value for any value of x_0. (This cubic equation does, in fact, have only one real root, $x = 2.3089\ldots$)

3 Proportion

Objectives

This is what you should be able to do after studying this chapter.

(1) Recognise that two sets of numbers $\{x\}$ and $\{y\}$ are in direct proportion if they can be connected by a relation of the form $y = kx$, where k is a constant number, and therefore represented by a linear graph through the origin.

(2) Interpret the statement '$y \propto x$' as being equivalent to '$y = kx$'.

(3) Understand and use the relations 'proportional to the square (cube) of' and 'inversely proportional to'.

(4) Draw linear graphs corresponding to the relations in (2) and (3).

Pre-test

1 (a) Plot the points $P(4, 3)$, $Q(8, 6)$, $R(10, 7.5)$ and $S(20, 15)$ on a graph and verify that they lie on a straight line through the origin.

(b) If $T(6, t)$ and $U(u, 12)$ also lie on this line, use your graph to find the values of t and u.

(c) Write down the equation of the line $PQRS$ in the form $y = kx$.

2 In the table below, the two variables x and y are related such that $y = 2.4x$. Find the values of j, k, l and m.

x	2	2.5	k	l	8
y	4.8	j	12	18	m

3 Copy and complete the tables for the following relations and draw the graphs of these relations.

(a) $y = 3x^2$

x	1	1.5			5	6.5	
y			12	27			192

(b) $xy = 36$

x	1	1.5	2	3	4	6	8	9
y								

3.1 Directly proportional sets

If you look at the x- and y-coordinates of the points described in question 1 of the Pre-test you can see that in each case the y-coordinate is three-quarters of the x-coordinate, and hence you were able to write down the relation $y = \frac{3}{4}x$ to show how the two sets of numbers $\{x\}$ and $\{y\}$ were connected.

In general terms, if two quantities A and B are such that as one changes, the other changes also in accordance with some simple relation, we say that

B varies with A (or *A varies with B*)

and *A and B are proportional to each other.*

(This latter statement may be expressed as

B is proportional to A, or *A is proportional to B*.)

If an increase in A corresponds to an increase in B, then the proportion (or proportionality) is said to be *direct*: if B decreases as A increases, then the proportion is said to be *inverse*.

In mathematical work, the word proportion is usually restricted to situations in which the relation is linear. Thus, in questions 1 and 2 of the Pre-test, y is directly proportional to x (and x is directly proportional to y), but not in part (a) of question 3.

Hence, mathematically,

$$B \text{ is directly proportional to } A \Leftrightarrow B = kA, \text{ for some constant } k.$$

In question 1 of the Pre-test, if we say that y is directly proportional to x, then the value of k is $\frac{3}{4}$. The number k is called the *constant of proportionality*; and if the x- and y-coordinates are considered as two ordered sets A and B, then A and B are described as *proportional sets*.

The notation for 'B is proportional to A' is $B \propto A$. (Think of this symbol as being halfway between the greek letter α and the symbol for infinity ∞.)

Thus $$B \propto A \Leftrightarrow B = kA, \text{ for some constant } k;$$

and $$[B \propto A \text{ such that } B = kA] \Leftrightarrow [A \propto B \text{ such that } A = \frac{1}{k}B].$$

For example, in question 1 of the Pre-test, as the graph is a straight line:

$$y \propto x \text{ such that } y = \tfrac{3}{4}x; \text{ and hence } x \propto y \text{ such that } x = \tfrac{4}{3}y.$$

1 Look at question 2 of the Pre-test. Are x and y directly proportional? Is y proportional to x? Is x proportional to y? If so, what are the constants of proportionality?

2 In question 3(a) of the Pre-test, let z stand for x^2 (i.e. $z = x^2$).
(a) Is $y \propto x$? Is $y \propto z$? Is $x \propto z$?
(b) For those pairs that are directly proportional, write down the value of k.

3 The variables C and r are directly proportional such that $r = 5$ when $C = 31$.

(a) What is the constant of proportionality if the relation is expressed in the form C is proportional to r? (In other words, what is the value of k if the relation is expressed as $C = kr$?)

(b) What is the value of k' (as a fraction) if the relation is written as $r = k'C$?

(c) Find the value of C when $r = 8$; and the value of r when $C = 15.5$.

2

Given one pair of members of the proportional sets A and B, and one member of a second pair, there are two ways of finding the second member of the second pair. These methods are shown in the two examples below, which expand the answer to part (c) of question 3 above.

Example 1. Figure 1 (a) shows the use of the proportional constant k.

From the given pair (5, 31) $k \times 5 = 31$, i.e. $k = \frac{31}{5} = 6.2$.

As the sets are proportional, $k \times 8 = x$ for the same value of k,

hence $x = 6.2 \times 8 = 49.6$.

Also $k \times y = 15.5$ for the same value of k,

hence $6.2 \times y = 15.5$

or $y = 15.5/6.2 = 2.5$.

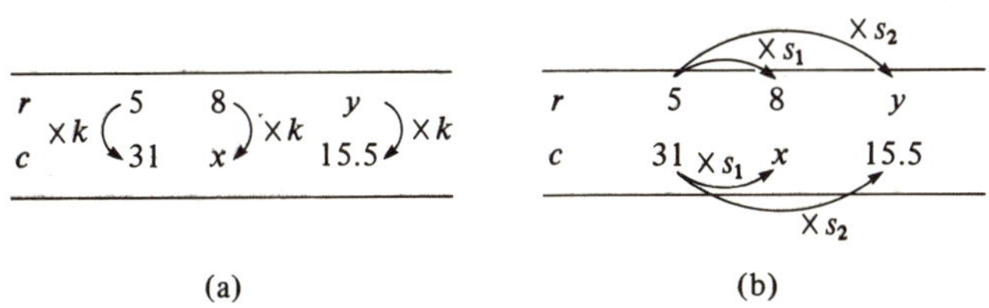

Figure 1

Example 2. Figure 1 (b) shows the use of a scale factor s.

As the sets are proportional, $s_1 \begin{bmatrix} 5 \\ 31 \end{bmatrix} = \begin{bmatrix} 8 \\ x \end{bmatrix}$.

Hence $s_1 \times 5 = 8$, i.e. $s_1 = 8/5 = 1.6$;

and $s_1 \times 31 = x$, from which $x = 1.6 \times 31 = 49.6$.

Also $s_2 \begin{bmatrix} 5 \\ 31 \end{bmatrix} = \begin{bmatrix} y \\ 15.5 \end{bmatrix}$.

Hence $s_2 \times 31 = 15.5$, i.e. $s_2 = 15.5/31 = 0.5$;

and $s_2 \times 5 = y$, from which $y = 0.5 \times 5 = 2.5$.

(Notice that the scale factor is different for different pairs.)

In any particular problem, use whichever method you find the more convenient. In the examples above it is perhaps slightly easier to use the k-method to find the value of x and the s-method to find the value of y.

If (A_1, b_1) and (A_2, b_2) are two corresponding pairs from proportional sets $\{A\}$ and $\{b\}$, Example 1 gives

$$b_1 = kA_1 \text{ and } b_2 = kA_2; \text{ i.e. } \frac{b_1}{A_1} = \frac{b_2}{A_2} = k \text{ or } \frac{A_1}{b_1} = \frac{A_2}{b_2} = \frac{1}{k}.$$

Example 2 gives

$$A_2 = sA_1 \text{ and } b_2 = sb_1; \quad \text{i.e.} \quad \frac{A_2}{A_1} = \frac{b_2}{b_1} = s \quad \text{or} \quad \frac{A_1}{A_2} = \frac{b_1}{b_2} = \frac{1}{s}.$$

These give us four variations of the relation between A_1, A_2, b_1, and b_2. The one that is usually quoted is

$$\frac{b_1}{A_1} = \frac{b_2}{A_2} = \frac{b_3}{A_3} = \ldots = k.$$

This allows the introduction of further corresponding pairs (such as (A_3, b_3), . . . , . . .) and the proportional constant k.

▷ **4** Use the method illustrated in Example 1 to find the values of x and y in the following pairs of proportional sets.

(a)

H	4	10	x
T	6	y	66.6

(b)

P	12	x	36
D	25	37.5	y

5 Repeat question 4 using the method illustrated in Example 2. ▶3

Exercise A

▷ **1** At a local garage, petrol cost 36 pence per litre (in 1982).

(a) How many litres of petrol (correct to two decimal places) could be bought for the following amounts of money?

£1, £2.25, £7.20, £P

(b) How much did it cost to buy the following amounts of petrol?

10 litres, 18 litres, 45.4 litres, L litres

(c) If L litres cost £P, write down a relation between L and P.

2 Given that y is directly proportional to x, complete the following table.

x	7	14	21	35	
y				45	54

3 Given that $y \propto x$, and that $y = 42$ when $x = 24$, find the constant of proportionality, and complete the following table.

x		16	24	48	
y	14		42		112

4 Figure 2(a) shows an unstretched spring, and Figure 2(b) shows the same spring - stretched when supporting a mass of 5 kg at its lower end.

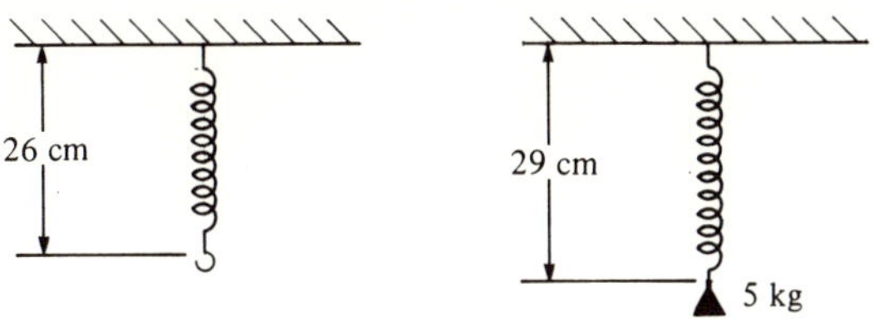

Figure 2

(a) How far has the mass of 5 kg stretched the spring? (That is, what is the extension in the spring?)

(b) If the extension of the spring is directly proportional to the mass that it supports, calculate the total length of the spring when it supports the following masses.

1 kg, 6 kg, 60 kg, 130 kg

(c) What mass will the spring be supporting when the extension is equal to the original length? 4

3.2 Some other proportional sets

In an experiment to find the lengths of pendulums that beat an exact number of seconds, a pendulum was formed by attaching a heavy mass at the end of a fine string. The times of swing for pendulums of various lengths were recorded as follows.

Length of pendulum (L cm)	50	100	150	200	250	300
Time taken for 1 swing (t sec)	1.4	2.1	2.5	2.9	3.3	3.6

1 (a) Draw a graph to show how t varies with L.

(b) Is the graph linear? Are $\{L\}$ and $\{t\}$ proportional sets?

(c) Copy and complete the following table.

Length (L cm)	50	100	150	200	250	300
$T = t^2$	2.0					

(d) Draw a graph to show how T varies with L, and deduce the lengths of pendulum required for swings of 1, 2, and 3 seconds. 5

The graph for part (d) of question 1 above gives an (approximate) straight line through the origin. This shows that (allowing for experimental error) $\{L\}$ and $\{T\}$ are proportional sets.

Thus $T \propto L$ or $T = kL$,

i.e. $t^2 \propto L$ or $t^2 = kL$.

Hence $t \propto \sqrt{L}$ or $t = k'\sqrt{L}$, where $k' = \sqrt{k}$.

We say that

'the square of the time is directly proportional to the length' ($t^2 \propto L$), or 'the time is directly proportional to the square root of the length' ($t \propto \sqrt{L}$).

The inverse relation is $L \propto T$ or $L = k''T$, where $k'' = \frac{1}{k}$,

i.e. $L \propto t^2$ or $L = k''t^2$.

This is read as

'the length is directly proportional to the square of the time'.

2 Find the values of k, k', and k'' in the above relations.

3 Describe the relation between y and x, and between x and y, in question 3(a) of the Pre-test. 6

Similar shapes

4 The following table shows the areas of circles with given radii.

Radius (r cm)	3	6	10	12	20
Area (A cm^2)	30	110	310	450	1260
(correct to the nearest 10 cm^2)					

(a) Is the area proportional to the radius?
(b) Using the figures in the table above, copy and complete this table.

Radius (r cm)	3
$R = r^2$	9
Area (A cm^2)	30

(c) Draw the graph of A against R. (That is, with the R-axis going across the page, and the A-axis going up the page.)
(d) Describe the relation between A and R, and hence between A and r. Write down a formula for A in terms of r. 7

Question 4 shows that, for any circle, the area is proportional to the square of the radius. In other words the sets $\{A\}$ and $\{r^2\}$ are proportional sets. Using the method of Example 2 in Section 3.1 we can therefore say that for any two circles

$$\text{ratio of areas} = (\text{ratio of radii})^2.$$

Circles are but one example of a set of geometrically similar shapes. In general, for any two similar shapes

$$\text{ratio of areas} = (\text{ratio of corresponding lengths})^2$$

i.e. $$\text{area factor} = \text{the square of the scale factor}.$$

Example 3. The corresponding sides of two similar triangles have lengths of 12 cm and 15 cm. If the area of the smaller triangle is 32 cm^2, find the area of the larger triangle.

Let the area of the larger triangle be A cm^2.

Then $\dfrac{A}{32} = \left(\dfrac{15}{12}\right)^2 = \left(\dfrac{5}{4}\right)^2 = \dfrac{25}{16}$ or 1.5625.

Hence $A = 32 \times 1.5625 = 50$;

the area of the larger triangle is 50 cm^2.

Further work on areas and volumes of geometrically similar shapes will be found in Chapter 1 of *Geometry 2: Shapes and Similarity*.

Exercise B

▷ 1 The quantities p and x are such that $p \propto x^2$, and $p = 5$ when $x = 4$.
(a) Find the value of p when $x = 8$.
(b) Write down a formula for p in terms of x.
(c) Find the value of p when $x = 7.6$, and the value of x when $p = 45$.

2 The relation between p and q in the following table is known to follow the 'square law'.

p	2	4	8	10
q	$\frac{1}{2}$	2	8	$12\frac{1}{2}$

(a) Copy the table above, and add on two lines to show the values of p^2 and q^2.
(b) Which is the correct relation: $p \propto q^2$ or $q \propto p^2$?
(c) By calculation or drawing find the constant of proportionality for the correct relation, and hence write down the formula connecting p and q. (Remember that if you draw the graph, the constant of proportionality is the gradient of the graph.) ▶ 8

▷ 3 The stopping distance of a car is proportional to the square of the speed at the moment when the brakes are applied.
If it takes 80 metres in which to stop when the speed is 100 km/h, in what distance will it stop when the speeds are 60 km/h and 120 km/h?

4 P_1, P_2, and P_3 are three regular pentagons of sides 8 cm, 10 cm, and 15 cm respectively. If the area of P_2 is 172 cm^2, calculate the areas of P_1 and P_3.

5 The base of a small cereal packet is a rectangle 16 cm by 10 cm, and the base of a larger packet is a rectangle 21 cm by 13 cm.
(a) Show that these rectangles are approximately similar (i.e. that they are approximately in proportion).
(b) The height of the smaller packet is 20 cm. If it is assumed that the two packets are similar in shape, calculate the height of the larger packet.
(c) If the larger packet holds 500 g when full, how much does the smaller packet hold? ▶ 9

3.3 Inverse proportion

1 The distance from London to New York is approximately 5600 km.

(a) If an aircraft travels at an average speed of 800 km/h, how long does it take to travel from London to New York?

(b) If the average speed is doubled, how long does it now take?

(c) Copy and complete the following table.

Average speed (v km/h)	400	500	700	800	1000	1200	1600
Time taken (t hours)							

(d) Draw the graph of t against v for $400 \leqslant v \leqslant 1600$. 10

This is an example of a situation involving two variables A and B in which B decreases as A increases. However, if we take the reciprocal of one of the variables (of A say), we now have a quantity that increases as B increases, and we investigate whether $\left\{\frac{1}{A}\right\}$ and $\{B\}$ are proportional sets.

2 (a) Copy and complete the following table, using the information given in question 1.

v	400	500	800	1000	1600
$\frac{1}{v}$			0.001 25		
t			7		

(b) Let $\frac{1}{v} = S$. Draw the graph of t against S, and write down its gradient.

(c) Hence write down a relation between t and v. 11

From parts (b) and (c) of question 2 we see that $t = 5600 \times \frac{1}{v}$.

In other words,

t is proportional to the reciprocal of v ($t \propto \frac{1}{v}$).

This is described as *inverse proportion*, and expressed as

t is inversely proportional to v.

3 Still using the information in question 1, copy and complete this table.

t	4	5	8	10	16
$\frac{1}{t}$					
v					

What do you notice? 12

Hence if t is inversely proportional to v, then it is also true that v is inversely proportional to t. In both cases, the constant of proportionality is the same. This leads us to a third way of expressing the relation between two sets (such as $\{ v \}$ and $\{ t \}$) that are inversely proportional:

the product of corresponding pairs is constant.

In the example of this section the product $vt = 5600$. More generally, if $\{ A \}$ and $\{ B \}$ are two sets that are inversely proportional, then

$$A_1B_1 = A_2B_2 = A_3B_3 = \ldots = k.$$

4 Boyle's law states that for a given amount (mass) of gas at a constant temperature, the pressure exerted by the gas is inversely proportional to the volume of the gas.

For a certain quantity of gas the pressure is 450 N/cm^2 when the volume is 100 cm^3.

(a) Find the volume of the gas when the pressure is 300 N/cm^2.

(b) Find the pressure exerted by the gas when it occupies a volume of 50 cm^3.

13

Exercise C

1 Copy and complete the following tables, given that y is inversely proportional to x. Express each relation in the form $xy = k$.

(a)

x	0.5	2	3	10
y			4	

(b)

x	1		5	200
y		20	8	

2 Complete the table below for the relation $xy = 24$.

x	1	2	3	4		8		24	48
y			8		4		2		

3 If a car starts from rest, and accelerates at a constant rate of a metres/second per second, then the time taken (t seconds) to reach a given speed is inversely proportional to the acceleration (a m/s^2).

If a car takes 6 seconds to reach a speed of 30 m/s when its acceleration is 5 m/s^2, find the time taken to reach the same speed when the acceleration is 4 m/s^2. What acceleration is necessary for the car to reach this speed in 3 seconds?

4 (The inverse square law)
One of the laws of gravity states that the gravitational force (F) between two bodies is inversely proportional to the square of the distance (d) between their centres of mass.

(a) Write this statement using the $\propto$ notation.

(b) If $F = 500$ when $d = 10$, calculate the value of F when $d = 5$, and the value of d when $F = 5$.

14

3.4 Graphs to show proportion

We have seen that if $y \propto x$,

then $\qquad y = kx$, for some constant k,

and the graph of y against x is a straight line through the origin, with gradient k.

1 (a) Given that 10 miles is approximately equal to 16.1 kilometres, draw a graph to show how distances measured in miles (I miles) vary with those same distances measured in kilometres (M kilometres) for $0 \leqslant I \leqslant 10$.

(b) From your graph find the equivalent distances to the following.

3 miles, 6.2 miles, 3 kilometres, 6.2 kilometres 15

As the graph is a straight line, it is possible to answer question 1 (b) reasonably accurately. It might therefore be useful if the other types of proportion could also be represented by straight line graphs. We have already done this in some cases, in fact.

Example 4. The table below shows the manufacturers' recommendations for the amount of fertiliser needed for fruit trees of various heights.

Height of tree (h m)	2	3	4	5	6
Mass of fertiliser (W kg)	0.14	0.32	0.57	0.90	1.30

Figure 3 (a) shows the graph of W against h. This looks like part of a parabola, which suggests that W is proportional to the square of h. For Figure 3 (b), therefore, we have plotted W against h^2. As this graph is approximately a straight line, our suggestion is confirmed.

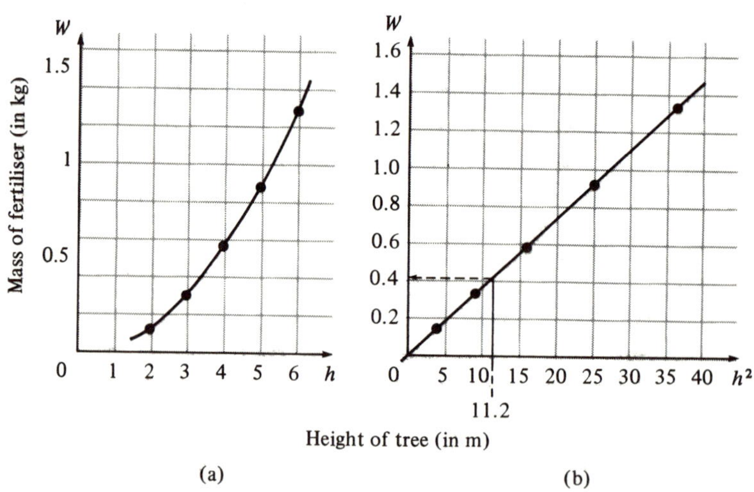

Figure 3

If we wish to find out how much fertiliser is required for a tree of, say, height 3.4 metres, we square 3.4 to give $h^2 = 11.6$ (correct to three significant figures), start at 11.6 on the h^2 axis (see Figure 3(b)), and read from the graph that $W = 0.42$.

Hence 0.42 kg of fertiliser are required.

2 (a) Use the data of question 3 of Exercise B to complete the following table.

Speed (v km/h)	0	60	100	120	200
v^2			10 000		
Stopping distance (d m)			80		

(b) From this information, draw the graph of d against v^2.
(c) From the graph estimate the stopping distance for a speed of 150 km/h.
(d) Use the graph to find the speeds, at the moments the brakes were applied, of cars that should stop in 50 m, 100 m, and 200 m. 16

For the inverse proportion situation in question 2 of Section 3.3 you obtained a straight line graph by plotting the time (t) against the reciprocal of the speed ($1/v$, which we called S). Look back at your answers to that question, and answer the following.

3 (a) Find the reciprocal of 600 and hence find the time taken when the average speed is 600 km/h.
(b) From your graph find the value of $1/v$ when $t = 5$. Find the reciprocal of this value, and hence find the average speed necessary for the journey to be completed in five hours. 17

Exercise D

1 (See question 1 of Exercise A.) Petrol costs 36p per litre.
Draw a graph to show the cost (£P) of L litres, for $0 \leqslant L \leqslant 50$, and use your graph to answer parts (a) and (b) of question 1 of Exercise A.

2 (a) For the data of question 2 of Exercise B, draw or sketch the following graphs.
q against p, q^2 against p, p^2 against q.
(b) How do these graphs help in answering part (b) of that question?

3 (a) Use your results to question 4 of Section 3.3 to draw a graph showing the relation between the pressure, P N/cm^2, and the volume, V cm^3, for $100 \leqslant V \leqslant 450$.
(b) By plotting a suitable function of the volume V, draw a straight line graph to show the same data.
(c) Use each graph to find the pressures corresponding to the the following volumes.

250 cm^3, 333 cm^3

(d) Use each graph to find the volume when the pressure is 250 N/cm^2. 18

Summary

(1) (a) Two (ordered) sets $\{x\}$ and $\{y\}$ are said to be directly proportional if all corresponding pairs (x, y) are connected by a relation of the form $y = kx$, where k is a constant.

(b) In such a case the graph of y against x is a straight line through the origin with gradient k.

(c) If $\{x\}$ and $\{y\}$ are proportional sets, then

y is proportional to x (this is written $y \propto x$),

and x is proportional to y ($x \propto y$).

(2) If $(x_1, y_1), (x_2, y_2), (x_3, y_3), \ldots$, are pairs of corresponding elements of two proportional sets, then

(a) $\dfrac{y_1}{x_1} = \dfrac{y_2}{x_2} = \dfrac{y_3}{x_3} = \ldots = k$;

(b) $\dfrac{y_1}{y_2} = \dfrac{x_1}{x_2}$, or $\dfrac{y_2}{y_1} = \dfrac{x_2}{x_1}$, etc.

(3) If two sets $\{x\}$ and $\{y\}$ are connected by a relation of the form $y = kx^2$, then y is directly proportional to the square of x ($y \propto x^2$).

(a) In such a case the graph of y against x is a parabola (see Figure 4(a)). If x^2 is replaced by X, then the graph of $y = kX$ is a straight line, i.e. the graph of y against x^2 is a straight line through the origin with gradient k (see Figure 4(b)).

(b) If $y \propto x^2$, then $x \propto \sqrt{y}$ (x is proportional to the square root of y).

(c) If $y \propto x^2$, then $\dfrac{y_2}{y_1} = \left(\dfrac{x_2}{x_1}\right)^2$, etc.

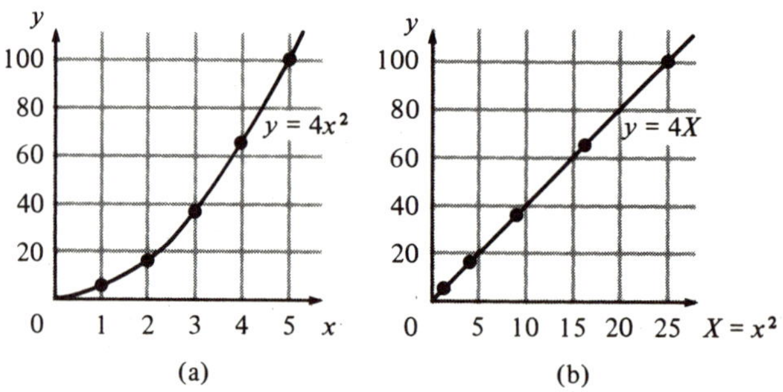

Figure 4

(4) (a) If two sets $\{x\}$ and $\{y\}$ are connected by a relation of the form $y = \dfrac{k}{x}$, then y is said to be inversely proportional to x.

(b) As the relation may be written as $y = k\left(\dfrac{1}{x}\right)$, another way of expressing this relation is to say that y is directly proportional to the reciprocal of x.

(c) Both methods of expression are written as $y \propto \dfrac{1}{x}$.

(d) If $y \propto \dfrac{1}{x}$, then $x \propto \dfrac{1}{y}$.

(e) If $y \propto \dfrac{1}{x}$, then $\dfrac{y_2}{y_1} = \dfrac{x_1}{x_2}$, etc.

(f) A third way of expressing such a relation is $xy = k$.

(g) The graph of y against x is shown in Figure 5(a). If the reciprocal of x is written as X (i.e. $X = \frac{1}{x}$) then the graph of $y = kX$ is a straight line through the origin. (See Figure 5(b).)

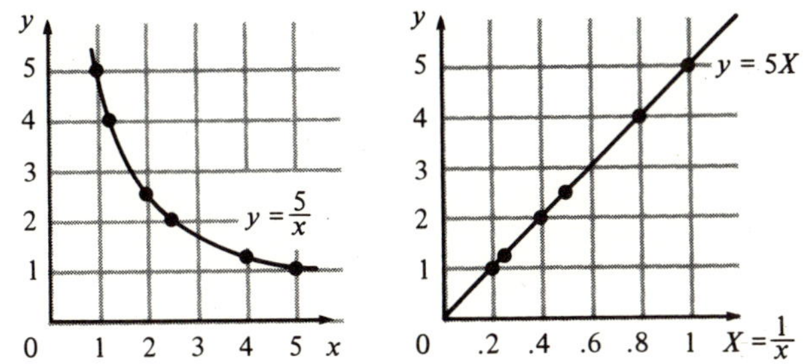

(a) (b) **Figure 5**

(5) (a) If two shapes are geometrically similar, then corresponding lengths are in direct proportion.

(b) If d_1 and d_2 are corresponding lengths in two similar shapes, such that $d_2 = kd_1$, and A_1 and A_2 are the areas of these shapes, then

$$\frac{A_2}{A_1} = \left(\frac{d_2}{d_1}\right)^2 = k^2,$$

i.e. area factor = (scale factor)^2.

Post-test

▷ 1 Sketch graphs for the following data. Which pairs of sets are directly proportional?

(a)

m	6	12	15	16.5
n	12	48	75	91

(b)

p	2	5	8	12
q	10	25	40	60

(c)

s	4	10	16	30
t	1	2.5	4	7.5

(d)

x	2	3	4	6
y	6	4	3	2

2 For each pair in question 1 that is not directly proportional, deduce the correct relation between the sets.

3 Given that $Z \propto T$, answer the following.

(a) Complete the following table.

T	2	5		15	18		24
Z		16	28.8	48		64	

(b) Write down the relation between Z and T.

4 The cost (£C) of buying negative film in bulk is directly proportional to the length (L metres) of film bought. If 30 metres cost £8.40, find

(a) the cost of 50 metres, and of 100 metres;

(b) the length of film (correct to the nearest metre) that can be bought for £5, and for £15.

5 Triangles PQR and XYZ are similar. (See Figure 6.)

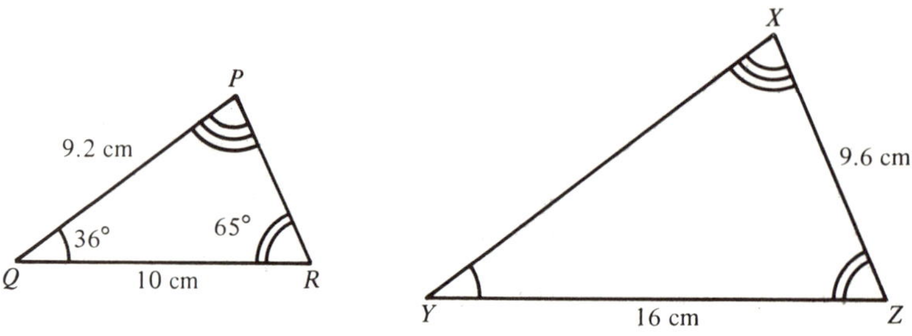

Figure 6

(a) State the sizes of the angles of triangle XYZ.

(b) Calculate, correct to one decimal place, the lengths (in cm) of PR and XY.

(c) Given that the area of triangle PQR is 27 cm^2 (correct to the nearest whole number of cm^2), calculate the area of triangle XYZ to the same degree of accuracy.

6 In an experiment, the following results were obtained.

t	0	10	20	30	40	50	60
C	0	25	36	44	52	57	62

The values of C were read correct to the nearest whole number, but it was suspected that one value of C was misread.

(a) Draw the graph of C against t.

(b) Which of the following graphs would you expect to be (approximately) linear?

C^2 against t, $\quad\sqrt{C}$ against t

(c) Draw the appropriate graph from (b) – or both! – and hence find whether any value of C was misread.

(d) Find the relation between C and t.

7 Determine which of the following pairs of sets are inversely proportional.

(a)

g	0.1	0.4	0.8	1.0
h	2.0	0.5	0.25	0.2

(b)

p	10	24	40	80
q	6	$2\frac{1}{2}$	$1\frac{1}{2}$	$\frac{3}{4}$

(c)

x	2.0	1.5	1.0	0.5
y	2.5	4.5	10	40

19 ▶

Assignment

1 Given that $y \propto x$, copy and complete the following table.

x		13		14	39
y	15	19.5	39		

2 Show that the sets $\{x\}$ and $\{y\}$ listed below are directly proportional, and write the relation between x and y in the form $y = kx$.

x	1.8	2.7	7.5	9.55	14.6
y	1.32	1.98	5.50	7.00	10.7

3 An American book on computing costs \$19.95. Find the cost in £, correct to the nearest 5p, for the following exchange rates.
(a) \$2.40 to the £ (b) \$1.70 to the £

4 Given that $y \propto 1/x^2$, complete the following table.

x	20	17	14		8
y		240		600	

5 It is given that y varies as the square root of x.
Which of the following graphs will be a straight line?
(a) y against x, (b) y against x^2, (c) y^2 against x, (d) y against $\sqrt{x}$

6 The values of x and y are related as shown in this table.

x	2	3	4	5
y	10	22.5	40	62.5

(a) Sketch the graphs of y against x, y against x^2, and y against $1/x$, and hence find the relation between x and y.
(b) Find the value of y (correct to one decimal place) when $x = 3.5$; and find the value of x (correct to one decimal place) that gives a value of 50 for y.

7 When a stone is dropped from the top of a high cliff, the distance through which it has fallen (d metres) is proportional to the square of the time (t seconds) for which it has been falling.
(a) It is known that after 2 seconds it has fallen through a distance of approximately 20 metres; and that it falls a distance of 100 metres in approximately $4\frac{1}{2}$ seconds.
Shown that this information is consistent with the original statement about proportionality.
(b) Find the relation between d and t.
(c) Find how far it falls in 10 seconds.
(d) Find how long it takes to fall 60 metres.

Answers

Pre-test

1 (a) See Figure A.
(b) See Figure A. The value of t is $4\frac{1}{2}$ and the value of u is 16.
(c) $y = \frac{3}{4}x$.

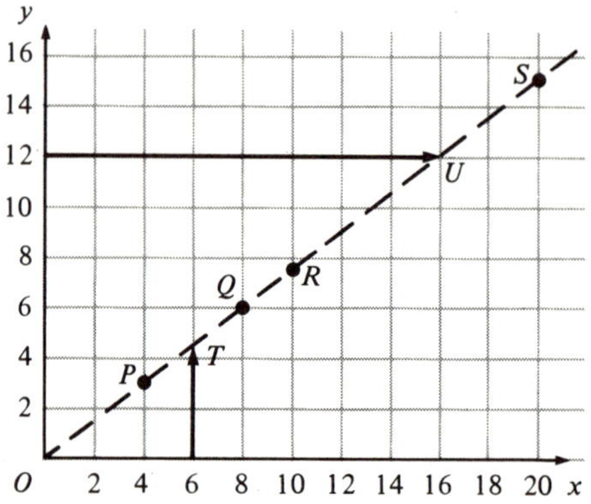

Figure A

2 $j = 2.4 \times 2.5 = 6$, $k = 12/2.4 = 5$, $l = 18/2.4 = 7.5$, $m = 2.4 \times 8 = 19.2$

3 (a)

x	(1)	(1.5)	2	3	(5)	(6.5)	8
y	3	6.75	(12)	(27)	75	126.75	(192)

See Figure B(a).

(b)

x	1	1.5	2	3	4	6	8	9
y	36	24	18	12	9	6	4.5	4

See Figure B(b).

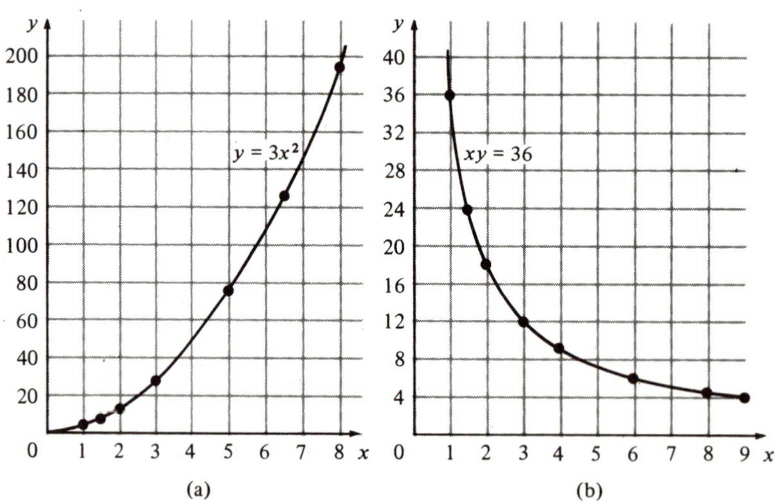

Figure B

3.1 Directly proportional sets

2 **1** x and y are directly proportional.
y is proportional to x such that $y = 2.4x$; i.e. $k = 2.4$ or $\frac{12}{5}$.
x is proportional to y such that $x = \frac{5}{12}y$; i.e. $k = \frac{5}{12}$.

2 (a) y is not proportional to x; y is proportional to z; x is not proportional to z.
(b) Since $y = 3z$, the value of k is 3.

3 (a) Let $C = kr$. Then $31 = k \times 5$, i.e. $k = 31/5 = 6.2$.
(b) Hence if $r = k'C$, $k' = 5/31$.
(c) If $r = 8$, then $C = 6.2 \times 8 = 49.6$.
If $C = 15.5$, then $r = \frac{5}{31} \times 15.5 = \frac{5}{31} \times \frac{31}{2} = 2\frac{1}{2}$.

3 **4** (a) $k = 6/4 = 1\frac{1}{2}$; $1\frac{1}{2} \times x = 66.6$ so that $x = \frac{2}{3}$ of $66.6 = 44.4$,
$1\frac{1}{2} \times 10 = y$ so that $y = 15$.
(b) $k = 25/12$; $\frac{25}{12} \times x = 37.5$ so that $x = \frac{12}{25} \times 37.5 = 18$,
$\frac{25}{12} \times 36 = y$ so that $y = 75$.

5 (a) If $s_1 \begin{bmatrix} 4 \\ 6 \end{bmatrix} = \begin{bmatrix} 10 \\ y \end{bmatrix}$, then $s_1 = 10/4 = 2\frac{1}{2}$, and $y = 2\frac{1}{2} \times 6 = 15$.

If $s_2 \begin{bmatrix} 4 \\ 6 \end{bmatrix} = \begin{bmatrix} x \\ 66.6 \end{bmatrix}$, then $s_2 = \dfrac{66.6}{6} = 11.1$, and $x = 11.1 \times 4 = 44.4$.

(b) If $s_1 \begin{bmatrix} 12 \\ 25 \end{bmatrix} = \begin{bmatrix} x \\ 37.5 \end{bmatrix}$, then $s_1 = \dfrac{37.5}{25} = 1\frac{1}{2}$, and $x = 1\frac{1}{2} \times 12 = 18$.

If $s_2 \begin{bmatrix} 12 \\ 25 \end{bmatrix} = \begin{bmatrix} 36 \\ y \end{bmatrix}$, then $s_2 = \dfrac{36}{12} = 3$, and $y = 3 \times 25 = 75$.

Exercise A

4 **1** (a) Volume $\propto$ cost, with a constant of proportionality of $\frac{1}{36}$ (litres per penny). Hence, to find the amount of petrol in litres, the amount of money in pence is multiplied by $\frac{1}{36}$.
The amounts are (correct to 2 d.p.) 2.78 litres, 6.25 litres, 20 litres, and $\dfrac{100P}{36}$ litres (or $2.78P$ litres).
(b) Cost is proportional to volume with a constant of 36 (pence per litre). To find the cost in pence, multiply by 36.
360 pence (£3.60), 648 pence (£6.48), 1634 pence (£16.34) to the nearest penny, $36L$ pence (or £$0.36L$).
(c) $L = \dfrac{100P}{36} = \dfrac{25P}{9}$ (= $2.78P$ approximately); or $P = 0.36L$.

2

x	(7)	(14)	(21)	(35)	42
y	9	18	27	(45)	(54)

The scale factor method is probably easier to use.

3

x	8	(16)	(24)	(48)	64
y	(14)	28	(42)	84	(112)

$y = \dfrac{7}{4}x$ or $x = \dfrac{4}{7}y$.

4 (a) A mass of 5 kg stretches the spring 3 cm.
(b) If extension ∝ mass, then extension = $\frac{3}{5}$ mass, or 0.6 × mass.

Mass	1 kg	6 kg	60 kg	130 kg
Extension	0.6 cm	3.6 cm	36 cm	78 cm
Total length	26.6 cm	29.6 cm	62 cm	104 cm

(c) Mass ∝ extension, such that mass = $\frac{5}{3}$ × extension.
Hence the mass required to produce an extension of 26 cm is $\frac{5}{3}$ × 26 kg = $43\frac{1}{3}$ kg.

3.2 Some other proportional sets

5 1 (a) See Figure C(a).
(b) The graph is not linear, and so $\{L\}$ and $\{t\}$ are not proportional sets.

(c)

Length (L)	50	100	150	200	250	300
t^2	2.0	4.4	6.2	8.4	10.9	13.0

(Values of t^2 are given correct to one decimal place.)
(d) See Figure C(b). This is a linear graph, approximately.

25 cm ($T = 1$), 95 cm ($T = 4$, i.e. $t = 2$), 210 cm ($T = 9$)
(All correct to nearest 5 cm.)

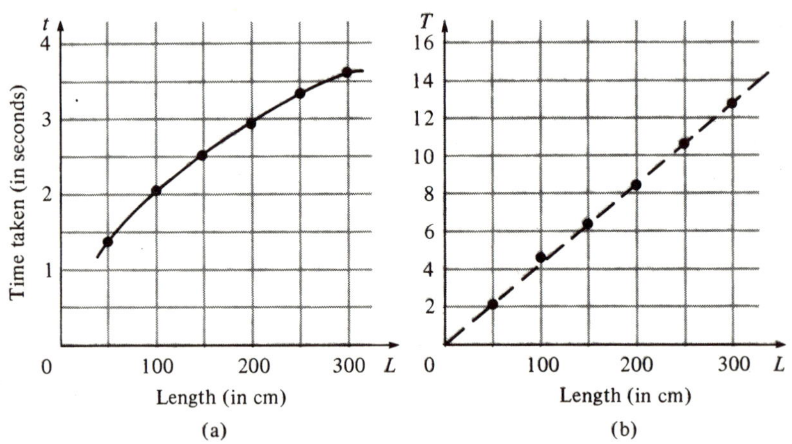

Figure C

6 2 From the graph in Figure C(b), when $L = 300$ then $T = 13$.
The gradient of the graph (and therefore the constant of proportionality) is $\frac{13}{300}$ (or approximately 0.043), and hence $T = 0.043L$ (approximately).
(Notice that as we have drawn the graph of T against L – i.e. L across the page, and T up the page – the equation of the line using the gradient worked out above is of the form 'T is a function of L'.)

For the inverse relation (L against T) the gradient will be the reciprocal of $\frac{13}{300}$

(i.e. $\frac{300}{13}$ or approximately 23) and the relation is $L = 23T$ (approximately).

Thus we have two ways of describing the relation between the length of the pendulum and its time of swing:

$$T = 0.043L, \quad \text{i.e. } t^2 = 0.043L \text{ or } t = \sqrt{(0.043L)} = 0.21\sqrt{L};$$

and $L = 23T$, i.e. $L = 23t^2$. (All the numerical constants are approximate.)

3 If $y = 3x^2$, then y is proportional to the square of x,
and x is proportional to the square root of y.

7 4 (a) The area is not (mathematically) directly proportional to the radius.

(b)

Radius (r cm)	3	6	10	12	20
$R = r^2$	9	36	100	144	400
Area (A cm^2)	30	110	310	450	1260

(c) See Figure D.

(d) A is proportional to R, and hence $A \propto r^2$.
From the table in part (b), or from the graph, the gradient of the graph of A against R is approximately 3.1; hence $A = 3.1r^2$, approximately. (The correct formula, of course, is $A = \pi r^2$.)

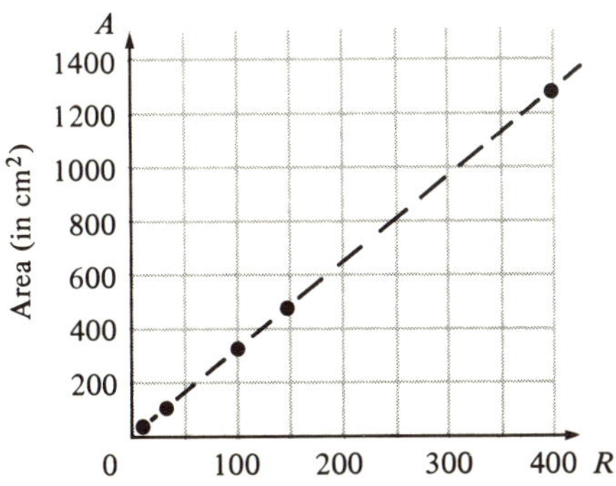

Figure D

Exercise B

8 1 If $p \propto x^2$, then $p = kx^2$ for some value of k.
Since $p = 5$ when $x = 4$, then $5 = k \times 4^2$; hence $k = \frac{5}{16}$.

(a) When $x = 8$, $p = \frac{5}{16} \times 8^2 = 20$.
(Alternatively: let $5 = p_1$, $4 = x_1$, and $8 = x_2$. Then, since $\frac{p_2}{p_1} = \left(\frac{x_2}{x_1}\right)^2$, $p_2 = 5 \times (\frac{8}{4})^2 = 20$.)

(b) $p = \frac{5}{16}x^2$.

(c) When $x = 7.6$, $p = 18.05$.
When $p = 45$, $x = 12$.

2 (a)

p	2	4	8	10
q^2	$\frac{1}{4}$	4	64	$156\frac{1}{4}$

q	$\frac{1}{2}$	2	8	$12\frac{1}{2}$
p^2	4	16	64	100

(b) From these tables you should see that $p^2 \propto q$, i.e. $q \propto p^2$.

(c) From the right-hand table, $p^2 = 8q$, or $q = \frac{1}{8}p^2$.

9 3 Let the stopping distance be d metres, and the speed be v km/h.

Then $d = kv^2$ such that when $v = 100, d = 80$. Hence $k = \frac{d}{v^2} = \frac{80}{10\,000} = 0.008$.

When $v = 60, d = 28.8$; and when $v = 120, d = 115.2$; hence the stopping distances are approximately 29 metres and 115 metres.

4 Let the lengths of the sides be d_1, d_2, and d_3 cm respectively; and the corresponding areas be A_1, A_2, and A_3 cm^2.

For similar figures, areas are proportional to the squares of the sides (all regular pentagons are similar to each other), hence

$$\frac{A_1}{(d_1)^2} = \frac{A_2}{(d_2)^2} = \frac{A_3}{(d_3)^2}.$$

Substituting 172 for A_2; 8 for d_1, 10 for d_2, and 15 for d_3; gives

$$A_1 = \frac{172 \times 64}{100} = 110.08 \quad \text{and} \quad A_3 = \frac{172 \times 225}{100} = 387.$$

The area of P_1 is about 110 cm^2, and the area of P_3 is 387 cm^2.

5 (a) For the smaller packet the ratio $\frac{\text{length}}{\text{width}} = \frac{16}{10} = 1.6$.

For the larger packet the ratio $= \frac{21}{13} = 1.61 \ldots$

Hence the bases of the packets are approximately similar.

Alternatively, the ratio of the lengths $= \frac{21}{16} = 1.3 \ldots$, and the ratio of the widths $= \frac{13}{10} = 1.3$. Hence the packets are approximately similar, with a scale factor of 1.3.

(b) The height of the larger packet will be about 1.3 × (the height of the smaller packet), or approximately 26 cm.

(c) As mass is proportional to volume, and volume is proportional to (length)^3, then

$$\text{mass} \propto (\text{length})^3$$

or

$$\frac{\text{smaller mass}}{\text{larger mass}} = \left(\frac{\text{smaller length}}{\text{larger length}}\right)^3.$$

Hence the smaller mass is approximately $(\frac{16}{21})^3 \times 500$ g, or $(\frac{10}{13})^3 \times 500$ g.
The first expression gives 221, correct to three significant figures, and the second 228, correct to three significant figures.
It would be reasonable to say that the mass of the smaller packet is 225 ± 5 g.
The packet would probably just be labelled 225 g!

3.3 Inverse proportion

10 1 (a) Time $= \frac{\text{distance}}{\text{speed}} = \frac{5600 \text{ km}}{800 \text{ km/h}} = 7$ hours.

(b) If the average speed is doubled, the time will be halved. It will now take $3\frac{1}{2}$ hours.

(c) Average speed (v km/h)	400	500	700	800	1000	1200	1600
Time taken (t hours)	14	11.2	8	7	5.6	4.7	3.5

(d) See Figure E.

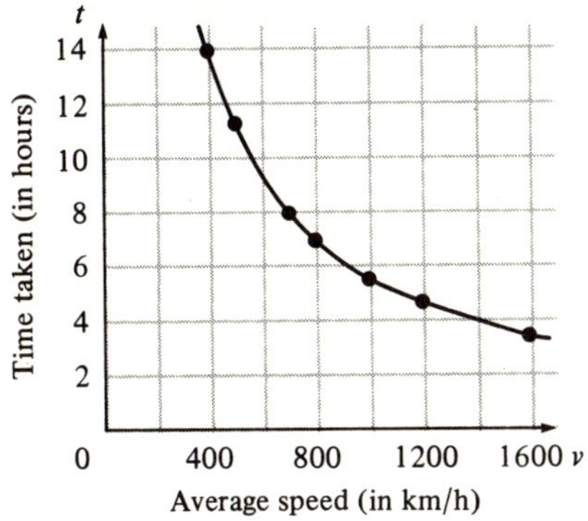

Figure E

11 2 (a)

v	400	500	800	1000	1600
$\frac{1}{v}$	0.0025	0.002	0.001 25	0.001	0.000 625
t	14	11.2	7	5.6	3.5

(b) See Figure F.
The gradient is 5600.

(c) The equation of the line is $t = 5600S$,

i.e. $t = 5600 \times \frac{1}{v}$ or $t = \frac{5600}{v}$.

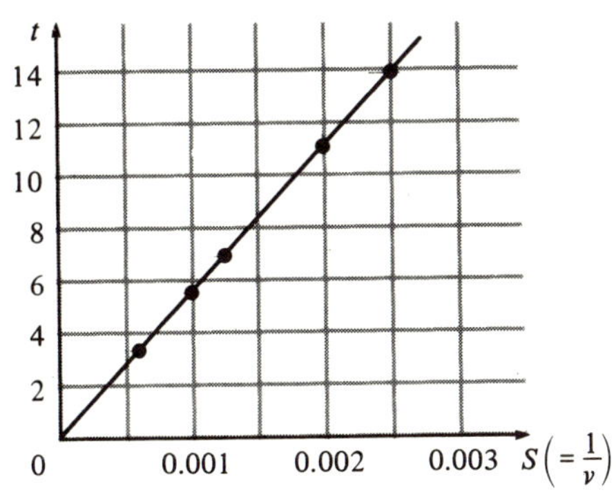

Figure F

12 3

t	4	5	8	10	16
$\frac{1}{t}$	0.25	0.2	0.125	0.1	0.0625
v	1400	1120	700	560	350

The graph of v against $1/t$ will be a straight line.

Hence v is proportional to $\frac{1}{t}$ (i.e. v is inversely proportional to t); and

$$v = 5600 \times \frac{1}{t} \quad \text{or} \quad v = \frac{5600}{t}.$$

13 4 If pressure is inversely proportional to volume, then the product of pressure and volume is constant. In this example the value of the constant is $450 \times 100 = 45\,000$.
(a) volume = 45 000/300 = 150 (cm^3) (b) pressure = 45 000/50 = 900 (N/cm^2).

Exercise C

14 1 (a)

x	(0.5)	(2)	(3)	(10)
y	24	6	(4)	1.2

$xy = 12$

(b)

x	(1)	2	(5)	(200)
y	40	(20)	(8)	0.2

$xy = 40$

2

x	(1)	(2)	(3)	(4)	6	(8)	12	(24)	(48)
y	24	12	(8)	6	(4)	3	(2)	1	0.5

3 Since time is inversely proportional to acceleration, then time $\times$ acceleration = constant (= increase in speed).
In this question the constant is 30; when the acceleration is 4 m/s^2, it will take $7\frac{1}{2}$ seconds; when the time taken is 3 seconds, then an acceleration of 10 m/s^2 will be necessary.

4 (a) $F \propto \frac{1}{d^2}$.

(b) Hence $F \times d^2$ is constant. In this example the constant = $500 \times 100 = 50\,000$.

Therefore $F = \frac{50\,000}{d^2}$. If $d = 5$, then $F = 2000$.

Also $d^2 = \frac{50\,000}{F}$. If $F = 5$, then $d^2 = 10\,000$, and so $d = 100$.

3.4 Graphs to show proportion

15 1 (a) See Figure G.
(b) See Figure G. 3 miles = 4.8 km, 6.2 miles = 10.0 km
3 km = 1.9 miles, 6.2 km = 3.8 or 3.9 miles
(These answers are given correct to one decimal place.)

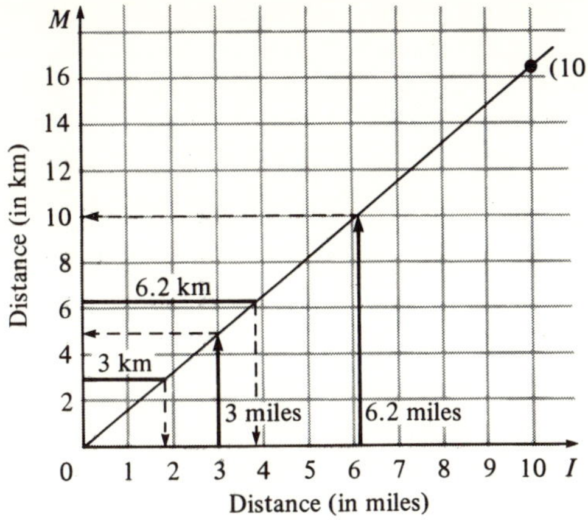

Figure G

16 2 (a)

v	0	60	100	120	200
v^2	0	3600	10 000	14 400	40 000
d	0	29	80	115	320

(b) See Figure H.
(The values for d are obtained from the answer to question 3 of Exercise B.)

(c) See Figure H. When $v = 150$, $v^2 = 22\,500$.
From the graph, when $v^2 = 22\,500$, $d = 180$.
The stopping distance is approximately 180 metres.

(d) See Figure H.

d	50	100	200	
v^2	6000	12 500	25 000	(read from the graph)
v	80	110	160	(from tables, correct to the nearest 10)

The speeds are approximately 80 km/h, 110 km/h, and 160 km/h.

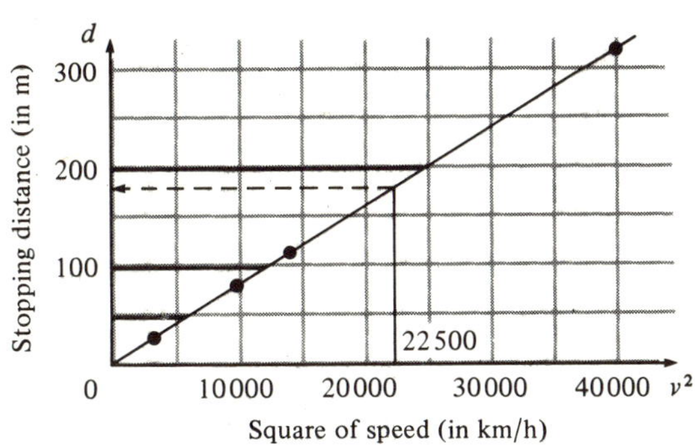

Figure H

17 3 (a) The reciprocal of 600 is 0.001 67 . . . .

From Figure F, when $\frac{1}{v} = 0.001\,67$, t is approximately 9.4.

When the average speed is 600 km/h, the time taken is approximately 9.4 hours.

(b) From Figure F, when $t = 5$, S (i.e. $\frac{1}{v}$) is approximately 0.0009.

Hence v is the reciprocal of 0.0009 = 1100 (approximately).
For the journey to be completed in 5 hours, the average speed should be about 1100 km/h.
(By calculation, the answer to (a) is about 9.3 hours, and the answer to (b) is about 1120 km/h.)

Exercise D

18 1 See Figure I. The graph will not be as accurate as calculation.

(a) The amounts of petrol can be read correct to the nearest litre, and are approximately 3 litres, 6 litres and 20 litres.

(b) The costs can be read to about the nearest 10p, and are approximately £3.60, £6.50, and £16.30 or £16.40.

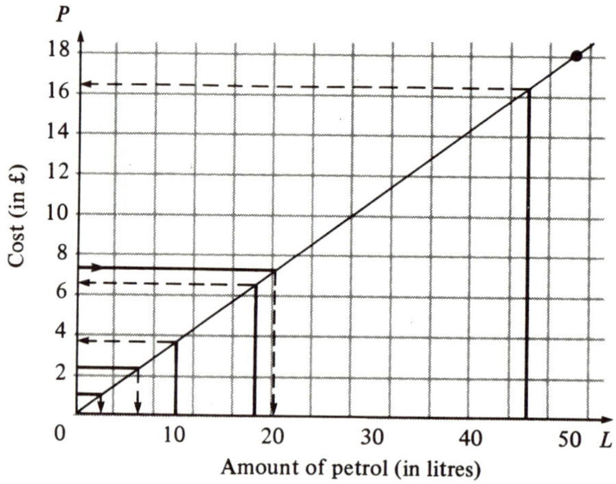

Figure I

2 (a) See Figure J.

(b) The graph that is approximately a straight line shows which two quantities are in direct proportion.

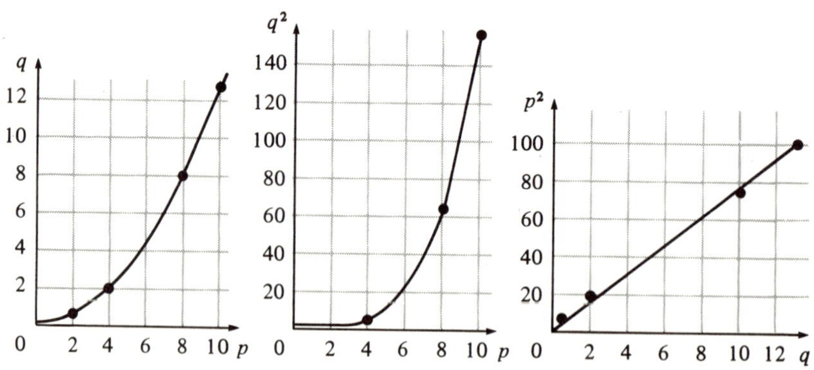

Figure J

3 (a) See Figure K(a).
(b) The 'suitable function' will be the reciprocal of the volume.

Volume (V cm^3)	100	150	300	450
$\frac{1}{V}$	0.01	0.0067	0.0033	0.0022
Pressure (P N/cm^2)	450	300	150	100

See Figure K(b).

(c) The pressures are approximately 180 N/cm^2 and 135 N/cm^2.
(When using Figure K(b), 1/250 = 0.004 and 1/333 = 0.003.)

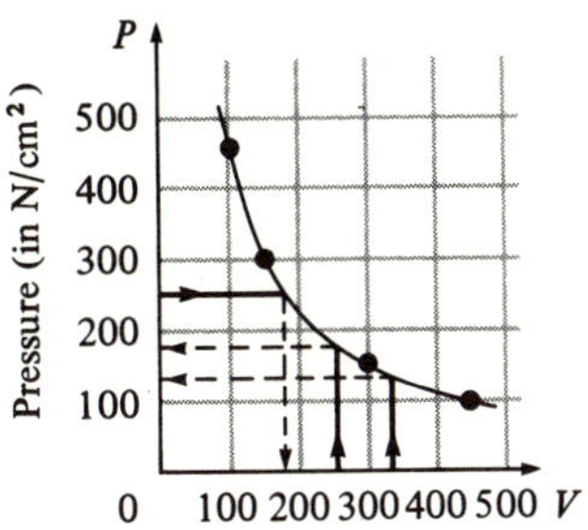

(a)

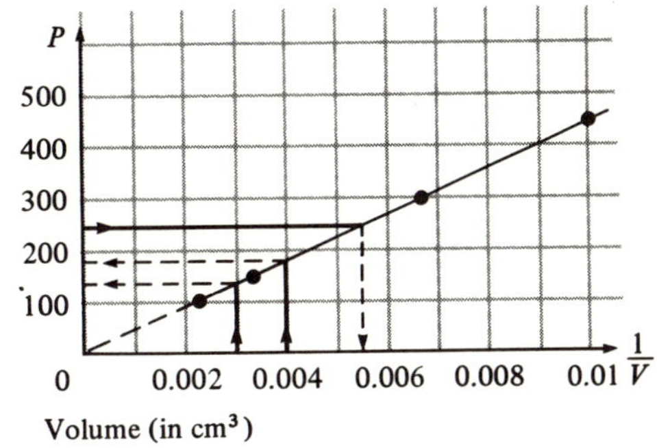

(b)

Figure K

(d) The volume is approximately 180 cm^3.
(From Figure K(b) $\frac{1}{V}$ = 0.0055. From reciprocal tables V is approximately 180.)

Post-test

19 1 See Figure L (page 88).
The sets $\{p\}$ and $\{q\}$ are directly proportional ($q = 5p$), and the sets $\{s\}$ and $\{t\}$ are directly proportional ($t = \frac{1}{4}s$, or $s = 4t$), as their graphs are straight lines through the origin.

2 For the sets $\{m\}$ and $\{n\}$, $n \propto m^2$ (or $m \propto \sqrt{n}$), such that $n = \frac{1}{3}m^2$ (or $m^2 = 3n$).
The sets $\{x\}$ and $\{y\}$ are inversely proportional; $y \propto \frac{1}{x}$ (or $x \propto \frac{1}{y}$) such that $xy = 12$.

3 (a)

T	2	5	9	15	18	20	24
Z	6.4	16	28.8	48	57.6	64	76.8

(b) $Z = 3.2T$ (or $Z = \frac{16}{5}T$), or $T = \frac{5}{16}Z$.

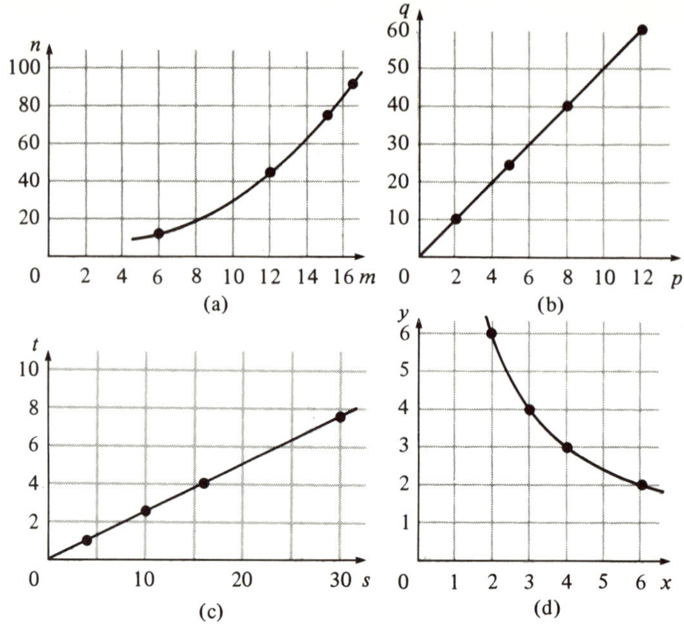

Figure L

4 Let $C = kL$. Then $8.4 = k \times 30$, which gives $k = \dfrac{8.4}{30} = 0.28$.

Hence $C = 0.28L$.

(a) The cost of 50 metres is £14, and the cost of 100 metres is £28.

(b) £5 will buy 18 metres, and £15 will buy 53 or 54 metres.

5 (a) The angles in both triangles are the same. Therefore angle $X = 79°$, angle $Y = 36°$ and angle $Z = 65°$.

(b) $\dfrac{PR}{9.6} = \dfrac{10}{16}$; hence $PR = 6.0$ cm.

$\dfrac{XY}{9.2} = \dfrac{16}{10}$; hence $XY = 14.7$ cm.

(c) Ratio of areas = (ratio of sides)^2 = $(16/10)^2 = 2.56$.

Area of triangle XYZ = 2.56 × area of triangle PQR

= 2.56 × 27 cm^2

= 69.12 cm^2 = 69 cm^2 (to nearest whole number).

6 (a) See Figure M.

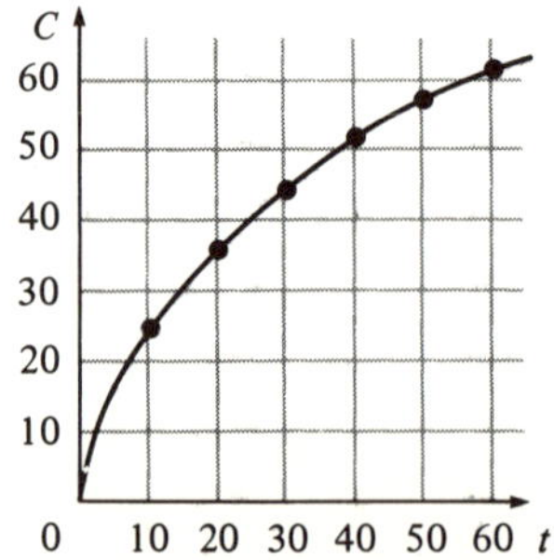

Figure M

(b) As the graph in part (a) is the 'inverse' to Figure L(a), then C^2 against t is more likely to give a straight line.

(c) Figure N shows both graphs.
Figure N(a) shows that the graph of C^2 against t is approximately linear. The scale of the printed graph is too small to be sure whether any value of C is misread. However, from the following table it can be seen that when $t = 40$, C should be less than 52. By trial, $C = 51$ fits in approximately with $C^2 = 64t$, or $C^2 = 65t$. ($C = 25$, for $t = 10$, also seems 'out'. However, if C were 26, $C^2/t = 67.6$, which is further 'out'.)

t	0	10	20	30	40	50	60
C	0	25	36	44	52	57	62
C^2	0	625	1296	1936	2704	3249	3844
$\frac{C^2}{t}$		62.5	64.8	64.5	67.6	65.0	64.1

(d) From Figure N(a) you should be able to deduce that $C^2 = 64t$ (or $C = 8\sqrt{t}$) approximately.

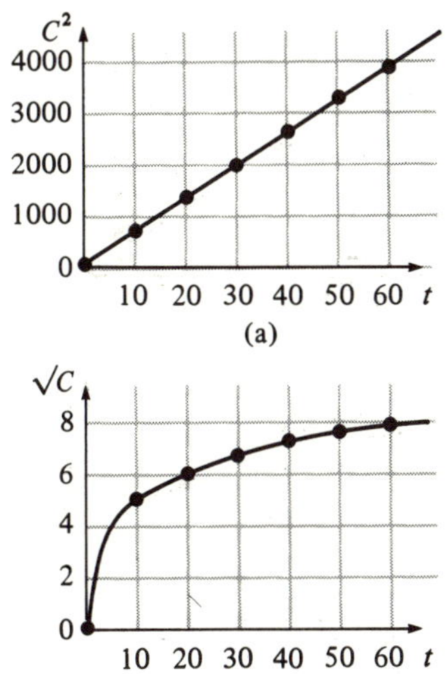

Figure N

7 If the sets $\{A\}$ and $\{B\}$ are inversely proportional, then the product of corresponding members is constant; i.e. $AB = k$.
(a) The values of gh are 0.2, 0.2, 0.2, and 0.2.
(b) The values of pq are 60, 60, 60, and 60.
(c) The values of xy are 5, 6.75, 10, and 20.
The sets $\{g\}$ and $\{h\}$ are inversely proportional, and the sets $\{p\}$ and $\{q\}$ are inversely proportional. (For the sets $\{x\}$ and $\{y\}$, $x^2y = 10$; and so x^2 is inversely proportional to y, or x is inversely proportional to $\sqrt{y}$ (or vice versa).)

4 Growth and decay

Objectives

This is what you should be able to do after studying this chapter.

(1) Recognise and use exponential functions of the form $f: x \to a^x$ for positive values of a.

(2) Apply the ideas of exponential functions to problems involving growth and decay of populations, etc.

(3) Calculate amounts of simple and compound interest.

Pre-test

1 (a) Copy and complete the table below for the function

$$f: x \to 1 + \frac{1}{10}x^2.$$

x	$^-3$	$^-2$	$^-1$	0	1	2	3	4	5	6
$f(x)$	1.9									

(b) Draw the graph of $y = 1 + \frac{1}{10}x^2$ for $^-3 \leqslant x \leqslant 6$.

2 (a) What does 6^3 mean? Find its value.

(b) Without using a calculator, find the values of the following.

5^4, $2^3 \times 2^7$, $3^{21} \div 3^{17}$, the cube root of 7^{12}, $(1.2 \times 10^5) \times (5 \times 10^{-4})$

(c) Use a calculator to evaluate the following correct to three significant figures.

1.5^{10}, 1.05^{10}, $16 \times (0.75)^8$, $250 \times (1.095)^5$

(d) Use a calculator to find, by trial and error, the smallest integral value of n for which $1.1^n > 2$.

4.1 Growth functions and their graphs

Growth functions

A good illustration of these functions is obtained by considering how some living things grow. The egg of a frog consists initially of a single cell. Once it has been fertilised, this cell divides into two. Each of these two cells then divides into two (giving a total now of four cells), each of these divides into two (giving a total of eight cells), and so on. If we write these numbers down in order, we obtain the sequence 1, 2, 4, 8, ...

1 (a) Write down the next three numbers (i.e. the 5th, 6th, and 7th terms) of this sequence.
(b) Express these three numbers as powers of 2.
(c) Write down the following numbers of the sequence.

10th, 12th, 21st, *n*th

2 If we assume that the divisions of these cells take place after equal intervals of time, we can make a table to show the number of cells at different times.
(a) Copy and complete the table below.

Time (t)	0	1	2	3	4	5	. . .	t
Number of cells	1	2 $= 2^1$	4 $= 2^2$	8 $= 2^3$				

(b) From this table, suggest a meaning for 2^0.
What would be the values of the following?

10^0, 12^0, x^0 (assuming that $x > 0$) 2

This sequence is an example of a growth function, and it can be written in the form

$$f: t \rightarrow 2^t.$$

At the moment it is defined only when t is a non-negative integer.

3 Write down the values of the following when $f: t \rightarrow 2^t$.
(a) $f(6)$ (b) $f(10)$ (c) $f^{-1}(128)$ (d) $f^{-1}(2048)$

4 For non-negative integral values of x the function q is defined by

$$q: x \rightarrow 5^x.$$

(a) Find the values of the following, using your calculator when necessary.

$q(0)$, $q(4)$, $q(5)$, $q(9)$, $q(16)$

(b) Find the value of q^{-1} (48 828 125), either by using the results of (a) above, or by successive division of 48 828 125 by 5. 3

The growth function that we have considered so far has been that for the number of cells from a frog's egg, and by the nature of the situation the range of the function (i.e. the number of cells) has been limited to positive integers, and the domain (i.e. the time) has been limited to non-negative integers. If we ignore the biological aspect, and consider this purely as a problem concerned with numbers and functions, is it possible to extend the function?

Some work has already been done in Chapter 1 on *Computation and Graphs*. Thus for non-positive integers we have results such as

$$2^0 = 1, \quad 10^0 = 1, \quad \text{and in fact } x^0 = 1 \text{ for all } x > 0;$$

$$2^{-3} = \frac{1}{2^3}, \quad 4^{-2} = \frac{1}{4^2}, \quad \text{and in general } a^{-n} = \frac{1}{a^n} \text{ for all positive integers } a \text{ and } n.$$

▷ **5** (a) Evaluate the following.

3^{-2}, 4^0, 5^{-3}, 8^{-3}, 9^0, 10^{-7}

(b) Use a calculator (and trial and error if necessary) to find the values of n for which 4^{-n} is equal to the following.

0.015 625, 0.000 976 562 5

6 (a) Copy and complete the following table.

t	$^-4$	$^-3$	$^-2$	$^-1$	0	1	2
2^t	0.06						
3^t	0.01						

(For negative values of t enter results correct to two decimal places.)

(b) Using one colour for values of 2^t and another colour for values of 3^t, plot these points on a graph. Do not join up the points yet!

(c) What can you say about the value of 2^{-n}, as the value of n becomes larger and larger?

4

The graph of a growth function

It is very tempting to join up the points on the graph that you have drawn for question 6, but does it make sense to do so? For the example quoted at the beginning of this section the answer is 'no'. It is not true to say that at a time of $2\frac{1}{2}$, for example, there were about 5 or 6 cells, or $5\frac{1}{2}$ cells!

However, in other situations the answer might be 'yes'. Look at Figure 1, which shows the population of a colony of bacteria at various hours before and after midday.

As we have a large population that is breeding quickly, it is now reasonable to assume that the population is increasing continuously. Thus, for example, it is reasonable to deduce from the graph that the population $2\frac{1}{2}$ hours after midday was approximately 5.7 million.

▷ **7** (a) From Figure 1 read off the populations (correct to the nearest 100 000) at the following times.

10.30 a.m., 11.30 a.m., 12.30 p.m., 1.30 p.m.

(b) From Figure 1 read off the approximate times at which the population was as follows.

0.8 million, 3 million, 6 million

5

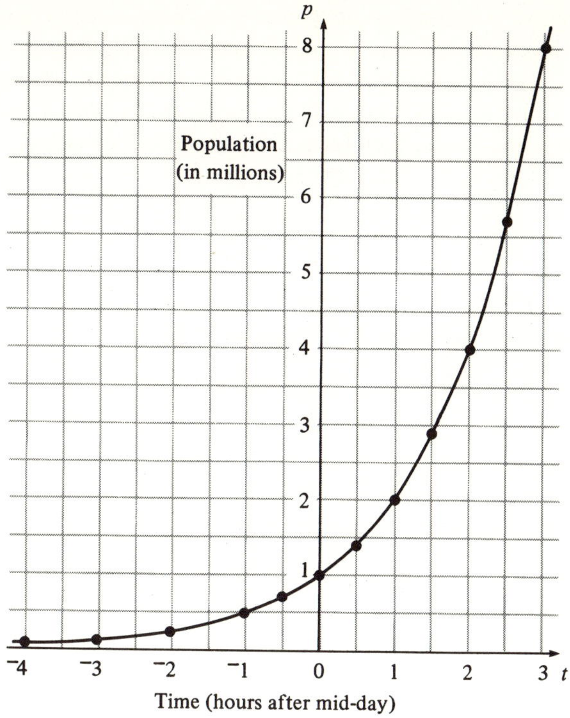

Figure 1

The exponential function

By drawing a continuous graph, as in Figure 1, we have suggested that a 'growth' function such as $f: t \rightarrow 2^t$ can be defined for all (real) values of t. The proper name for such a function is *exponential*. In the expression 2^t the number 2 is called the *base*, and the number t is called the power, or index, or *exponent*. Hence if f is a function in which the variable (x, or t, etc.) occurs as the index or exponent of a (constant) base, then f is described as an *exponential function*.

So far the bases of our exponential functions have been (positive) integers. It is not difficult to see that our definition can be extended again.

8 (a) Use your calculator to evaluate (correct to two decimal places) values of $(1.1)^x$ for $x = {}^-4, {}^-3, \ldots 2$.

(Remember that $(1.1)^{-1} = \frac{1}{1.1}$, $(1.1)^{-2} = \frac{(1.1)^{-1}}{1.1}$, etc.)

(b) Show these results on a graph.

9 Repeat question 8 for the function

$$f: x \rightarrow (2.5)^x.$$

6

In questions 8 and 9, although you were asked to plot points for integral values (of x) only, you were probably tempted to draw a curve through the points, and again it seems reasonable to do so. If your calculator has a $\boxed{y^x}$ (or equivalent) button, you can verify that the calculator considers this a reasonable operation to do. Check, for example, that

$(1.1)^{2.4}$ – that is, 1.1 raised to the 'power' 2.4 – has a value of approximately 1.26; and that 2.5 to the power $^{-}1.2$ has a value of approximately 0.33.

In the later sections of this chapter we use 'continuous' (i.e. defined for all values of x, not just integral values) exponential functions in which the base is a positive number, but not necessarily an integer. Such functions provide mathematical models for growths and decays of populations, amounts of money, etc.

Exercise A

1 A growth function is defined by $g: x \to 3^x$.
Write down the values of the following.

$g(2)$, $g(5)$, $g(0)$, $g(^{-}3)$, $g^{-1}(3)$, $g^{-1}(243)$

2 A population function is defined by $p: t \to 500(1.08)^t$, for $t \geqslant 0$, where t is the time in years.
(a) Calculate the values of $p(t)$ for $t = 0, 1, 2, 3, \ldots, 9$.
(b) Draw a graph to show the function p for $0 \leqslant t \leqslant 9$.
(c) From your graph estimate the times at which the population has the following values.

600, 700, 800, 900 7

4.2 Decay functions

The half-life of the radioactive element thallium is about 4 minutes. This means that over *any* interval of 4 minutes half the mass of the thallium changes (decays) into another element (in this case, lead). Thus if we start with 1.00 g of thallium, then after an interval of 4 minutes there will be 0.50 g of thallium, and 0.50 g of lead. After another 4 minutes there will be 0.25 g of thallium (and 0.75 g of lead), and so on.

1 (a) Copy and complete the table below.

Time (minutes)	0	4	8	12	16	20
Mass of thallium (g)	1.00	0.50	0.25			

(b) After 2 minutes it was found that the mass of thallium was approximately 0.71 g. Make a table similar to that in part (a) to show the mass at times of 6, 10, 14 and 18 minutes.

2 (a) Use the results of question 1 to draw a graph to show the mass (m grams) after a time of t minutes.
(b) Find from your graph the mass of thallium after 1 minute. 8

You should notice that the graph is similar to that drawn in Section 4.1, but 'reversed' – i.e. reflected in the y-axis. The way in which the mass of the thallium is changing is similar to the way in which the number of cells of the frog changes; but instead of doubling in a certain time (as do the number of cells in the frog) the mass of thallium is being halved in a certain time. We describe this as a *decay function*.

3 From question 2(b) you should have found that the mass of thallium after 1 minute was approximately 0.84 g. Copy and complete the following table. (Record all your results correct to two decimal places.)

Time (t minutes)	0	1	2	3	4	5	6	7	8
$(0.84)^t$	1	0.84	0.71						

(To find each value, multiply the preceding entry by 0.84.) 9

Comparing these results with questions 1 and 2, we see that the decay function for thallium is of the form

$$d\colon t \to (0.84)^t$$

i.e., after t minutes the mass of thallium is $(0.84)^t$ grams. Thus this sort of decay function is exponential as well, but with a base a whose value is between 0 and 1.

4 The area of a certain wood is being decreased each year by one fifth. (This is done by clearing the requisite area in the December of each year.)

(a) What fraction of the original wood remains after the first clearing? The first clearance took place in December 1980. If the area of the original wood was 750 ha, calculate the area of woodland remaining on the 1st January 1981 and on the 1st January 1982.

(b) Copy and complete the table below. (Enter the areas correct to the nearest hectare.)

Year (1980 = 0)	0	1	2	3	4	5	6	7	8	9	10
Area on the 1st Jan. (ha)	750	600									

(c) How long does it take for the original area to be halved?

(d) When does the actual decrease first become less than 40 ha per year? 10

Exercise B

1 The half-life of radium C is 20 minutes. At time $t = 0$ the mass of a quantity of radium C is 1.00 g.

(a) Calculate the mass of radium C remaining after 1 hour, 2 hours, and 3 hours.

(b) Calculate the approximate time taken to decay to a mass of 1 mg. (1 mg = 0.001 g.)

(c) Find the value of a if the mass of radium C after t hours is a^t grams.

2 The table below gives the estimated population of butterflies on Newsea Heath on the 1st July of each year.

Year (1975 = 0)	0	1	2	3	4	5	6
Population	1000	830	690	570	470	390	325

(a) Show these results on a graph. Does this look like an exponential decay function?

(b) Assuming that the decay is exponential, estimate the population in 1984; and the year in which the population will first be less than 100. 11

4.3 The exponential function

So far we have considered the exponential function in the form $y = a^x$. This has meant that when $x = 0$, y has had to be 1. But the original value, or *initial value*, of y (whether it be a population, mass, area, etc.) is not usually 1, and so it is necessary to extend the exponential function.

1 (a) Copy and complete the table below for $y = 5 \times 2^x$.

x	$^{-}2$	$^{-}1$	0	1	2	3	4
2^x	$\frac{1}{4}$		1		4		
y	$1\frac{1}{4}$		5		20		

(b) Draw the graph of $y = 5 \times 2^x$ for values of x from $^{-}2$ to 4.

(c) From your graph read off the values of y when $x = 1.5, 2.5$, and 3.5. 12

It should be obvious that we obtain the same sort of growth graph, and that this is still a growth function that doubles itself for each unit increase in x. This time, however, the initial value of y is 5. Thus a more general form of the exponential function is

$$y = ka^x$$

where k is the initial value of y, and a is the base, or growth factor.

We shall now look at two worked examples that illustrate the exponential function. In the first example the base is a number greater than 1, and so we shall refer to it as a growth factor. In the second example the population is decreasing. This can occur only if the base is a number less than 1; we shall refer to this as a decay factor.

Example 1. At the beginning of a year, 36 m^2 of the surface of a lake was covered with a pondweed. If left unchecked, the area covered by the pondweed increases by 2% each month (i.e. for any month, the area covered at the end of the month is 2% more than the area covered at the beginning of that month).

Calculate the area that will be covered by the pondweed by the end of the year if the growth is not checked.

During the first month the area increases by 2%, so that at the end of this month the total area covered will be

$$\begin{aligned} & 36 \text{ m}^2 + 2\% \text{ of } 36 \text{ m}^2 \\ = \; & 100\% \text{ of } 36 \text{ m}^2 + 2\% \text{ of } 36 \text{ m}^2 \\ = \; & 102\% \text{ of } 36 \text{ m}^2 \\ = \; & 1.02 \times 36 \text{ m}^2 \\ = \; & 36.7 \text{ m}^2 \text{ (to 3 s.f.).} \end{aligned}$$

During the second month the increase will be 2% of 36.7 m^2, so that at the end of this month the total area covered will be

$$\begin{aligned} & 36.7 \text{ m}^2 + 2\% \text{ of } 36.7 \text{ m}^2 \\ = \; & \ldots \\ = \; & 1.02 \times 36.7 \text{ m}^2 = 37.4 \text{ m}^2 \text{ (to 3 s.f.).} \end{aligned}$$

But 36.7 is the result of calculating 1.02 x 36. Hence an alternative expression for calculating the area covered after two months is

$$1.02 \times (1.02 \times 36)\,\text{m}^2$$
$$= (1.02)^2 \times 36\,\text{m}^2.$$

Similarly the total area covered by the end of the third month will be

$$1.02 \times 37.4\,\text{m}^2$$
$$= 1.02 \times [(1.02)^2 \times 36]\,\text{m}^2$$
$$= (1.02)^3 \times 36\,\text{m}^2.$$

Hence the total area covered after n months will be

$$(1.02)^n \times 36\,\text{m}^2 \quad \text{or} \quad 36 \times (1.02)^n\,\text{m}^2.$$

Thus this is an exponential growth function. The initial value is 36, and the growth factor is 1.02 (taking 1 month as the unit of time).

The total area covered after 12 months is found by putting $n = 12$. This gives

$$36 \times (1.02)^{12}\,\text{m}^2$$
$$= 45.\dot{6}\ldots\,\text{m}^2 \text{ (or } 46\,\text{m}^2 \text{ correct to the nearest whole number).}$$

Example 2. The population of a small village over a number of years was as follows.

Year	1977	1978	1979	1980	1981
Population	420	385	355	325	300

Show that the change in population is approximately exponential; and estimate what the population was in 1971, and what it will be in 1991, if the pattern remains exponential.

The decay factor for 1977 to 1978 was $\frac{385}{420} = 0.92$ (to 2 s.f.), and the decay factors for the following three years were $\frac{355}{385} = 0.92$, $\frac{325}{355} = 0.92$, and $\frac{300}{325} = 0.92$ (all correct to 2 s.f.). As these factors are all the same, we can say that the change was exponential for the years 1977 to 1981, with decay factor 0.92. In other words,

population in any year = 0.92 x (population in the previous year).

To find the estimated population in 1991 we continue multiplying by 0.92; that is, we multiply 300 by 0.92 another ten times. Hence the estimated population in 1991 is

$$300 \times (0.92)^{10} = 130 \text{ (to 2 s.f.)}.$$

To estimate what the population was in 1971 we work backwards from the 1977 figure, dividing by 0.92 six times.

$$420 \div (0.92)^6 = 690 \text{ (to 2 s.f.)}.$$

Note that in the first part of Example 2 we are effectively taking 1981 as year 0, and using 300 as the 'initial' population. On this basis 1991 is year 10, and so the estimated population in 1991 is $300 \times (0.92)^{10}$; 1971 is year $^{-}10$, and so the estimate for the population in 1971 could have been evaluated from $300 \times (0.92)^{-10}$. In the second part of the example we used 1977 as the initial year (and hence used 420 as the initial population). On this basis 1971 is year $^{-}6$; and 1991 is year 14. Hence an alternative expression for the estimated population in 1991 is $420 \times (0.92)^{14}$. These alternative expressions do, of course, given the same results as previously.

▷ 2 The pondweed on the lake described in Example 1 is now controlled so that the area it covers is decreased by 2% each month.
(a) State the decay factor.
(b) If the area covered at the beginning of a year is 36 m^2, calculate the area still covered at the end of 12 months.
(c) How long does it take for the area covered to be halved? 13

▷ 3 In Example 2 above, take 1979 as year 0, and find the following.
(a) The population function in the form $p: t \rightarrow ka^t$.
(b) The estimated population in the year 1991.
(c) An estimate of the population in 1971. 14

Exercise C

▷ 1 The table below shows how many of the cars of a certain make, all manufactured in 1970, were still roadworthy in the years 1977–1982.

Year	1977	1978	1979	1980	1981	1982
No. of roadworthy cars	2670	2000	1500	1120	840	630

(a) Show that the percentage decrease from 1977 to 1978 was 25.1%, correct to three significant figures.
(b) Calculate the percentage decreases for the following years. Is this an exponential function?
(c) Estimate the number of cars likely to be roadworthy in 1984.
(d) In what year will the number of roadworthy cars first be less than 100?
(e) Estimate how many cars of this make were originally manufactured in 1970.

2 A new town was built at Goodtown in 1975 with an initial population of 60 000. The growth of this town is controlled so that the population increases by approximately 3% each year.
(a) Taking 1975 as year 0, write down the formula for the estimated population, p people, in year t.
(b) Estimate the size of the population in 1984 if this rate of growth is maintained.
(c) In what year will the population reach 100 000? 15

4.4 Money

Simple interest

'Interest rates now 8.75% p.a.'

What does this statement mean? If you had invested £100 on the 1st April 1980 (through a bank or building society, for example), how much money would you have been able to withdraw one year later, on the 1st April, 1981? Since '*per cent*' means in (or for) *every hundred*, then every £100 earns £8.75 interest. The abbreviation 'p.a.' stands for '*per annum*', which is the Latin for *each year*, and so every £100 earns £8.75 interest each year. Thus the original investment of £100 would have earned £8.75 in interest after one year, and on the 1st April 1981 you would have been able to withdraw a total amount of £108.75.

If you had originally invested £300, then – as the rate of interest is 8.75% – the total interest after 1 year would be 3 x £8.75, or £26.25. Hence the total amount after 1 year (original investment + interest) would be £326.25.

1 Find the interest from, and the total amount of, the following investments after 1 year.
   (a) £100 invested at 10.5% p.a.
   (b) £1000 invested at 12.3% p.a.
   (c) £60 invested at 8% p.a.
   (d) £2400 invested at 9.25% p.a.

16

The other factor in an interest rate is that it is 'per annum'. This means that while the sum of money remains invested, it earns interest every year. Thus the £300 invested on the 1st April 1980 would earn £26.25 interest in the year that ended on the 31st March 1981, a further £26.25 interest in the year 1st April 1981 to 31st March 1982, a further £26.25 interest in the year 1st April 1982 to 31st March 1983, and so on. Hence after 5 years (for example) the total interest earned would be 5 x £26.25, or £131.25.

If the interest is quoted as 'simple interest', then only the original sum of money earns any interest. If, in the example quoted above, you left the original sum of £300 invested for 5 years, you could receive your interest in five annual (yearly) payments of £26.25, or as one payment of £131.25 at the end of the five years. (In many cases it is also possible to receive the interest at more frequent intervals. For the example above this could be half-yearly payments – i.e. payments every 6 months – of £13.12$\frac{1}{2}$; or monthly payments of $\frac{1}{12}$ of £26.25.)

These ideas are contained in the 'Simple Interest formula'

$$I = \frac{PRT}{100}$$

which gives the interest earned (I) on an original sum (or *principal*) of P, when invested at a rate of R% for a period of time T. The sums of money I and P must be in the same units (usually £s), and the unit of time in R and T must be the same (usually years).

Example 3. Find the simple interest, and the total amount, when £350 is invested for 4 years at a rate of 9.5% p.a.

Here $P = 350$, $R = 9.5$, and $T = 4$, and as P is measured in £s, then the interest I will also be measured in £s. Substitution in the formula gives

$$I = \frac{350 \times 9.5 \times 4}{100} = 133,$$

hence the interest is £133, and the total amount is £350 + £133 = £483.

The time for which the money is invested does not always have to be a whole number of years, and many financial institutions will pay interest for a fraction of a year on a proportional basis.

Example 4. Find the simple interest on £2000 when invested for 20 months at a rate of 18% p.a.

$P = 2000$, $R = 18$, and $T = \frac{20}{12}$. (Note that the time must be expressed in years as the rate is so much *per annum*.) Substitution in the formula gives

$$I = \frac{2000 \times 18 \times 20}{100 \times 12} = 600,$$

hence the total interest earned after 20 months is £600.

▷ 2 Find the simple interest on the following investments.
(a) £500 for 3 years at 7.9% p.a.
(b) £42 for $2\frac{1}{2}$ years at 8.5% p.a.
(c) £6000 for 4 months at 16% p.a.
(d) 72p for 2 months at 25% p.a.

17 ▶

Compound interest

In practice, most rates of interest are 'compound'. This means that the interest (provided it is not withdrawn) itself earns interest. In other words, at the end of the first year (or whatever unit of time is used) the interest earned during that year is added on – or *compounded* – to the original sum invested, so that the 'principal' at the beginning of the second year is the original sum of money invested plus the interest earned in the previous year. During the second year, interest is paid on all this sum; and at the end of the second year this interest is compounded to the 'principal'. Such interest is compounded at regular intervals determined by the nature of the investment. The commonest intervals of time for compounding interest are daily, monthly, half-yearly (i.e. every six months), and yearly.

Example 5. On the 1st September 1980 a sum of £500 was invested at a rate of 9.5% p.a., interest to be compounded annually, for a period of 3 years. If no interest is withdrawn during the three years, calculate the total value of the investment on the 1st September 1983.

Original investment (1.9.1980)	=	£500.00
Interest added on (31.8.1981) = 9.5% of £500	=	£ 47.50
Total value of investment at the end of the first year	=	£547.50

This interest is compounded to the original sum of £500 to give a new 'principal' of £547.50. As the interest is compounded, all of this earns interest in the next year.

Amount invested (1.9.1981)	=	£547.50
Interest added on (31.8.1982)		
= 9.5% of £547.50	=	£ 52.01
Total value of the investment at the end of the second year	=	£599.51

All of this earns interest in the third year;

i.e. interest added on (31.8.1983)		
= 9.5% of £599.51	=	£ 56.95
Total value of the investment at the end of the third year	=	£656.46

Notice that under compound interest the amount of interest increases each year (£47.50 in the first year, £52.01 in the second year, £56.95 in the third year, in the example above), and the increases themselves are getting larger (the second year's interest was an increase of £4.51 on the first year's interest, and the third year's interest was an increase of £4.94 on the second year's interest).

The type of calculation illustrated in Example 5 would become tedious (even with a calculator) if the investment period were 10, or 20, years! But since the interest added at the end of any year is always the same percentage of the total investment at the beginning of that year, we have another example of an exponential growth. In Example 5, the unit of time is 1 year, and the initial amount is 500 (£s). As the interest that is added on is 9.5% of the amount at the beginning of any year, the total amount at the end of that year will be 109.5% of the amount at the beginning of the year; i.e. the growth factor is 1.095.

Hence a formula for the total amount (£A) after a time of t years is

$$A = 500 \times (1.095)^t.$$

3 (a) Verify that when $t = 2$ and $t = 3$ this formula gives the same results as in Example 5 above.

(b) Calculate the total value of the investment after 10 years if the same rate of compound interest is maintained. 18

If the interest is compounded at a different unit of time a little more care is required, but the method of calculating the interest and the total value of the investment is similar.

Example 6. Another sum of £500 was invested on the 1st September 1980 at a rate of 9.5% p.a., for a period of 3 years; but this time the interest is to be compounded half-yearly (i.e. every six months). Calculate the value of this investment at the end of the three-year period.

A rate of 9.5% p.a. is equivalent to a rate of 4.75% every six months; and a period of 3 years is equivalent to a period of 6 half-years. Hence, this time, interest at the rate of 4.75% has to be compounded (to the total value of the investment at the beginning of each half-year) six times.

Original investment (1.9.1980)	= £500.00
Interest added on (28.2.1981)	
= 4.75% of £500	= £ 23.75
Value of investment (1.3.1981)	= £523.75
Interest (4.75% of £523.75)	= £ 24.88
Value of investment (1.9.1981)	= £548.63
Interest	= £ 26.06
Value of investment (1.3.1982)	= £574.69
Interest	= £ 27.30
Value of investment (1.9.1982)	= £601.99
Interest	= £ 28.59
Value of investment (1.3.1983)	= £630.58
Interest	= £ 29.95
Value of investment (1.9.1983)	= £660.53

You should realise that this is again exponential, but this time the unit of time is half a year, and the growth factor is therefore 1.0475. Notice that Example 6 is a better investment than Example 5!

4 (a) Verify the answer to Example 6 by substituting 6 for t in the formula

$$A = 500 \times (1.0475)^t.$$

(b) Calculate the total value of this investment after 10 years if the same rate of interest continues to be compounded half-yearly. Compare this result with part (b) of question 3 above. 19

Exercise D

1 In practice, many building societies pay interest half-yearly on the 30th June and the 31st December, irrespective of when the investment started.

£500 is invested on the 1st September 1980, at a rate of 9.5% p.a., for a period of three years, the interest being compounded half-yearly on the 30th June and the 31st December of each year.

(a) Calculate how much interest is earned in the four months September to December 1980, and hence the total value of the investment on the 1st January 1981.

(b) Calculate the value of the investment on the 1st July 1983.
(Take the value of the investment on the 1st January 1981 as the initial value, and apply the growth factor for a half-year unit of time – i.e. 1.0475 – five times.)

(c) Calculate the interest on this amount for the two months July and August 1983, and hence find the total value of the investment on the 1st September 1983.

2 Some banks compound interest on a daily basis.

(a) Express an interest rate of 9.1% p.a. as a rate per day, correct to four decimal places. (Not a leap year!)

(b) Write down an expression to show the total value of £500 after one year when the interest is compounded daily.

(c) If you can, evaluate this expression correct to the nearest penny, and compare the result with the value of the investment in Example 5 after one year. (If you have an $\boxed{y^x}$ button on your calculator, or if you can use a combination of calculator and logarithms, it is easy. Otherwise ingenuity, or much hard work, is required!) 20

Summary

(1) (a) A function $x \to f(x)$ is exponential if $\dfrac{f(x+1)}{f(x)} = a$, where a is a (positive) constant, for all values of x.

(b) If $a > 1$, then $f(x)$ is increasing as x increases. The constant a is sometimes called the growth factor.

(c) If $a < 1$, then $f(x)$ is decreasing as x increases. In this situation the constant a is sometimes called a decay factor.

(d) If the initial value of $f(x)$ is k (i.e. if $f(0) = k$), then an exponential function may be written in the form

$$f: x \to ka^x.$$

(2) If the rate of growth (population, area, money, etc.) is proportional to its present size, then the growth is exponential.

For example, if the population of a town is increasing at the rate of 5% per year (i.e. in any one year the population increases by 5% of its value at the beginning of that year), and if $p(t)$ is the population at the end of year t, then

$$\begin{aligned} p(t+1) &= p(t) + 5\% \text{ of } p(t) \\ &= 105\% \text{ of } p(t) \\ &= 1.05 \times p(t). \end{aligned}$$

Hence $\dfrac{p(t+1)}{p(t)} = 1.05$, which is constant, and so the growth is exponential.

If P is the initial population, then $p(t) = P \times (1.05)^t$.

(3) (a) To test whether a set of figures corresponds to an exponential function, use the definition in (1)(a).

(b) To find how long it takes for a population to double/halve itself, etc., work out successive values of $f(1), f(2), f(3), \ldots$, (multiply $f(0)$ repeatedly by the growth factor a) until a result is obtained.

(c) To find the initial value (given, say, $f(4)$ and the growth factor a), work backwards as shown below.

Since $f(4) = f(0) \times a^4$,
then $f(0) = f(4) \div a^4$,
i.e. divide $f(4)$ by a four times to find $f(0)$.

(4) *Simple interest*. The simple interest on £400 invested for 30 months (= $2\frac{1}{2}$ years) at $7\frac{1}{2}$% p.a. (i.e. $7\frac{1}{2}$% per year) is

$$\frac{£400 \times 2.5 \times 7.5}{100} = £75.$$

The total value of the investment (the amount) after $2\frac{1}{2}$ years would therefore be £400 + £75 = £475.

(5) *Compound interest*. When the interest is left with the original investment so that the interest itself also earns interest, the interest is said to be compounded. In such cases the growth of the value of the investment is exponential.

(a) A rate of interest of 7% p.a. compounded (added) yearly is equivalent to a growth factor of 1.07, as after the first year the new value of the investment is 107% of the original, or 1.07 × (the original value). If the original investment was £A, then the total value of the investment after t years is

$$£A \times (1.07)^t.$$

(b) A rate of 7% p.a. compounded half-yearly (i.e. interest is added on to the original investment every six months) is equivalent to a rate of 3.5% every six months. In this case the total value of the investment after t years (i.e. after $2t$ half-years) is

$$£A \times (1.035)^{2t}.$$

Post-test

1 During the breeding season, the number of redfly doubles every eight days. At the beginning of the season (day 0) the number in a certain garden was 1000.

(a) Write down the formula for P (the population of redfly on day t) in terms of t and the growth factor a.

(b) Substitute 2000 for P, and 8 for t, and hence obtain an equation for a. By using the relation $((a^2)^2)^2 = a^8$, or otherwise, find the value of a (to 3 s.f.).

(c) Calculate the population at the end of a breeding season that lasted for 50 days.

(d) During the non-breeding season, 99% of the flies die off. How long should the breeding season have lasted in order for the population at the beginning of the next breeding season to be at least 1000?

2 A sum of £1000 is invested at 12% p.a. for a period of 9 months.

(a) Calculate the simple interest on this investment.

(b) Calculate the interest if it is compounded every three months.

(c) Calculate the interest if it is compounded daily.

3 The area of 'wetlands' in a certain county has decreased in recent years as shown by the table below.

Year	1975	1976	1977	1978	1979	1980
Area (ha)	490	430	375	330	290	255

(a) Show that the decay is approximately exponential, and find the decay factor.
(b) Estimate the area that will be 'wetlands' in 1984.
(c) When will the area of 'wetlands' first be less than 100 ha?
(d) When was the area of 'wetlands' last more than 1000 ha? 21

Assignment

1 In an evaporation experiment the following results were obtained.

Volume of liquid remaining (cm^3)	1000	900	800	700	600	500	400	300
Time (minutes)	0	$2\frac{1}{2}$	5	8	$11\frac{1}{2}$	16	21	27

(a) Draw a graph to show the volume of liquid as a function of the time (i.e. draw the time axis across the page).
(b) Show that the rate of evaporation with respect to time is approximately exponential, and calculate the decay factor.
(c) Calculate the time taken for 90% of the liquid to evaporate.

2 With some building societies the phrase 'withdrawal at 3 months' notice' means that your investment earns no interest for the last three months before you withdraw it.
A person intends to invest £3000 for a period of 2 years. Calculate the total interest earned in the following situations.
(a) A share account (for which no notice of withdrawal is required) paying 8.6% compounded every six months.
(b) A share account paying 8.8% compounded annually.
(c) A '1 months' notice of withdrawal' account paying 9% compounded every six months.
(d) A '3 months' notice of withdrawal' account paying 10% compounded annually.

Answers

Pre-test

1 1 (a)

x	$^-3$	$^-2$	$^-1$	0	1	2	3	4	5	6
$f(x)$	1.9	1.4	1.1	1	1.1	1.4	1.9	2.6	3.5	4.6

(b) See Figure A.

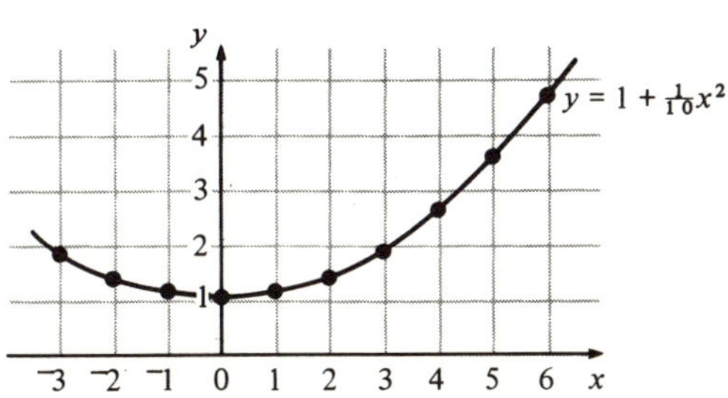

Figure A

2 (a) 6^3 means 'six cubed', i.e. $6 \times 6 \times 6$. $6^3 = 216$.

(b) 625, 2^{10} (= 1024), 3^4 (= 81), 7^4 ($= 49^2 = 2401$) since 7^4 cubed $= 7^4 \times 7^4 \times 7^4 = 7^{12}$, $(1.2 \times 5 \times 10^1) = 60$.

(c) $(1.5)^2 = 2.25$; $(1.5)^4 = (2.25)^2 = 5.0625$; $(1.5)^8 = (5.0625)^2 = 25.6289\ldots$;
hence $(1.5)^{10} = 25.6289\ldots \times 2.25 = 57.665\ldots = 57.7$ (to 3 s.f.).
$(1.05)^{10} = 1.62889\ldots = 1.63$ (to 3 s.f.).
$16 \times (0.75)^8 = 1.6018\ldots = 1.60$ (to 3 s.f.).
$250 \times (1.095)^5 = 393.5596\ldots = 394$ (to 3 s.f.).

(d) $(1.1)^7 = 1.948\ldots$; $(1.1)^8 = 2.143\ldots$; hence $n = 8$.

4.1 Growth functions and their graphs

2 1 (a) 16, 32, 64.

(b) 2^4, 2^5, 2^6.

(c) The tenth number is $2^9 = 512$. The other numbers are $2^{11} = 2048$, $2^{20} = 1048576$, and 2^{n-1}

2 (a)

Time (t)	0	1	2	3	4	5	...	t
Number of cells	1	2 $= 2^1$	4 $= 2^2$	8 $= 2^3$	16 $= 2^4$	32 $= 2^5$		2^t

(b) This suggests that the value of 2^0 is 1.
Similarly $x^0 = 1$ for any value of $x > 0$.

3 3 (a) $2^6 = 64$ (b) $2^{10} = 1024$ (c) 7 (since $2^7 = 128$)
(d) 11 (since $2^{11} = 2048$)

4 (a) 1, $5^4 = 625$, $5^5 = 3125$, $5^9 = 1953125$, $1.5258\ldots \times 10^{11}$
(b) 11 (since $5^{11} = 48828125$)

4 5 (a) $1/3^2 = 1/9$, 1, $1/5^3 = 1/125$, $1/8^3 = 1/512$, 1, $1/10^7$
(As decimals the answers are 0.111 . . . , 1, 0.008, 0.001 953 125, 1, and 0.000 000 1.)

(b) $4^{-3} = 0.015625$, $4^{-5} = 0.00097656$

6 (a)

t	$^{-}4$	$^{-}3$	$^{-}2$	$^{-}1$	0	1	2
2^t	0.06	0.12	0.25	0.5	1	2	4
3^t	0.01	0.04	0.11	0.33	1	3	9

(b) See Figure B.

(c) As n becomes larger and larger the value of 2^{-n} becomes smaller and smaller, but it is never quite zero.

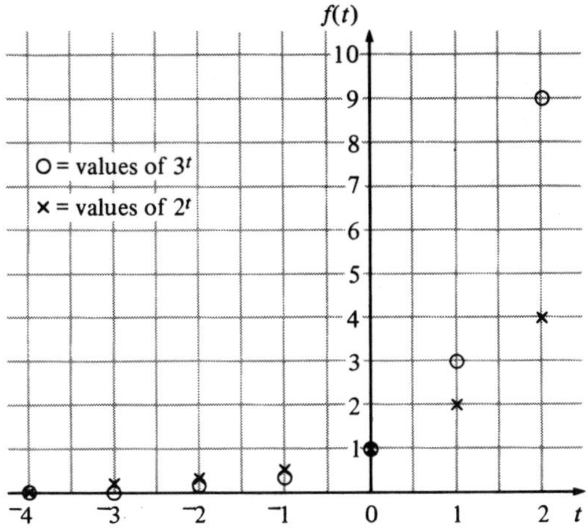

Figure B

5 **7** (a) 10.30 a.m. is $^{-}1\frac{1}{2}$ hours after midday. When $t = {}^{-}1\frac{1}{2}$, $p = 0.3$ (million). The population (in millions) at the other times are as follows:

0.7, 1.4, 2.8.

These figures show that the population takes an hour to double itself, no matter at what time that hour starts. (For example, if the population at 1.15 p.m. is 2.3 million, then one hour later, at 2.15 p.m., the population will be 4.6 million.)

(b) 11.45 a.m., 1.35 p.m., 2.35 p.m.

6 **8** (a)

x	$^{-}4$	$^{-}3$	$^{-}2$	$^{-}1$	0	1	2
$(1.1)^x$	0.68	0.75	0.83	0.91	1	1.1	1.21

(b) See Figure C.

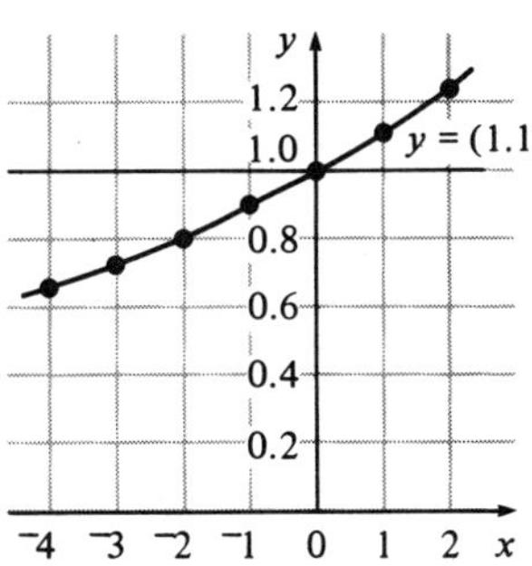

Figure C

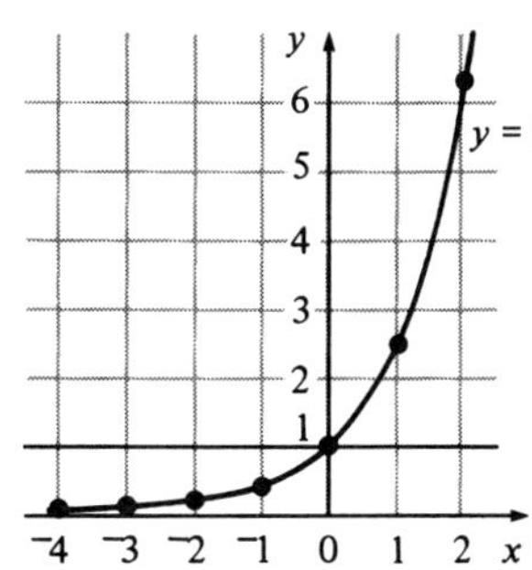

Figure D

9 (a)

x	$^{-}4$	$^{-}3$	$^{-}2$	$^{-}1$	0	1	2
$(2.5)^x$	0.03	0.06	0.16	0.4	1	2.5	6.25

(b) See Figure D.

Exercise A

7 1 $g(2) = 9$, $g(5) = 243$, $g(0) = 1$, $g(^{-}3) = 3^{-3} = \frac{1}{3^3} = \frac{1}{27}$ (= 0.037...),
$g^{-1}(3) = 1$ (since $3^1 = 3$), $g^{-1}(243) = 5$ (since $3^5 = 243$)

2 (a)

t	0	1	2	3	4	5	6	7	8	9
$p(t)$	500	540	583	630	680	735	793	857	925	1000

(Values of $p(t)$ are given correct to the nearest whole number.)

(b) See Figure E.

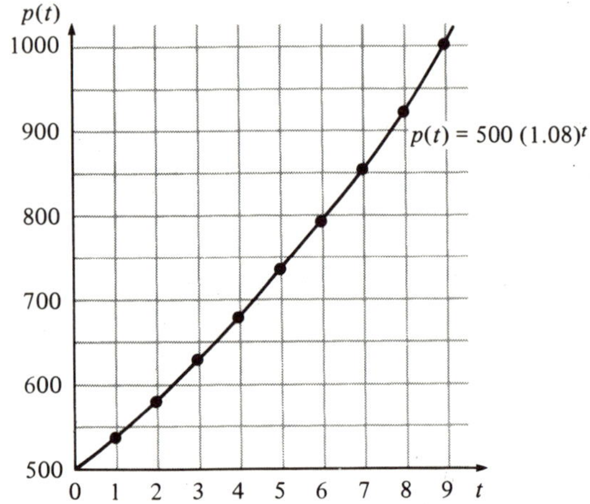

Figure E

(c)

Population	600	700	800	900
Time (years)	2.4	4.4	6.1	7.6

(Values of t are given correct to one decimal place.)

4.2 Decay functions

8 1 (a)

Time (minutes)	0	4	8	12	16	20
Mass (g)	1.00	0.50	0.25	0.12	0.06	0.03

(b)

Time (minutes)	2	6	10	14	18
Mass (g)	0.71	0.36	0.18	0.09	0.04

2 (a) See Figure F.

(b) Approximately 0.84 g.

9 3

t	0	1	2	3	4	5	6	7	8
$(0.84)^t$	1	0.84	0.71	0.59	0.50	0.42	0.35	0.30	0.25

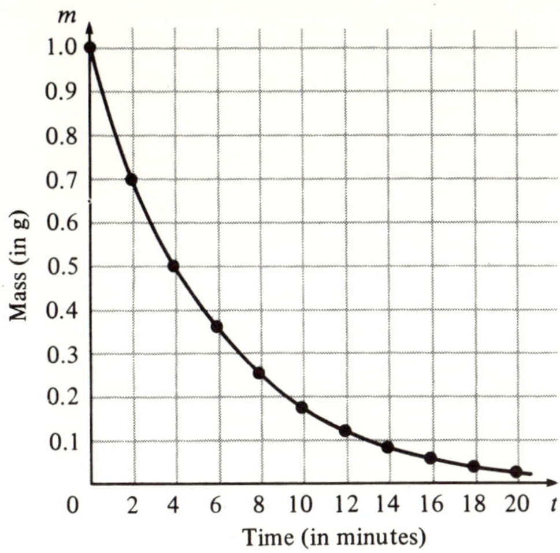

Figure F

10 4 (a) The fraction remaining is $\frac{4}{5}$.
Hence the area of woodland on the 1st January 1981 is $\frac{4}{5} \times 750$ ha = 600 ha.
The area of woodland on the 1st January 1982 is $\frac{4}{5} \times 600$ ha = 480 ha.

(b)

Year	0	1	2	3	4	5	6	7	8	9	10
Area	750	600	480	384	307	246	197	157	126	101	81

(c) After 3 years the area is 384 ha, therefore it takes just over 3 years for the area to be halved (i.e. from 750 ha to 375 ha).

(d) In 1986 (year 6) the actual decrease will be 40 ha. Therefore in year 7 (1987) the annual decrease will first fall below 40 ha per year.

Exercise B

11 1 (a) After 1 hour (= 3 x 20 minutes) the mass of radium left is $(0.5)^3$ g = 0.125 g.
After 2 hours the mass remaining is $(0.5)^6$ g [i.e. $(0.125)^2$ g] = 0.016 g approximately.
After 3 hours the mass remaining is $(0.125)^3$ g = 0.002 g approximately.

(b) After 3 hours the mass remaining is approximately 0.002 g.
This mass will be halved in a further 20 minutes, as the 'half-life' is 20 minutes.
Hence the time taken to decay to a mass of 1 mg is approximately 3 hours 20 minutes.

(c) As the original mass at time $t = 0$ is unit mass (1 g), the value of a in the function

$$m: t \to a^t \text{ (where } m(t) \text{ is the mass after } t \text{ hours)}$$

is given by the mass at time $t = 1$.
After 1 hour, the mass of radium left is 0.125 g.
Hence the mass at time t (hours) is given by the function

$$m: t \to (0.125)^t.$$

2 (a) See Figure G. The graph does appear to be exponential.

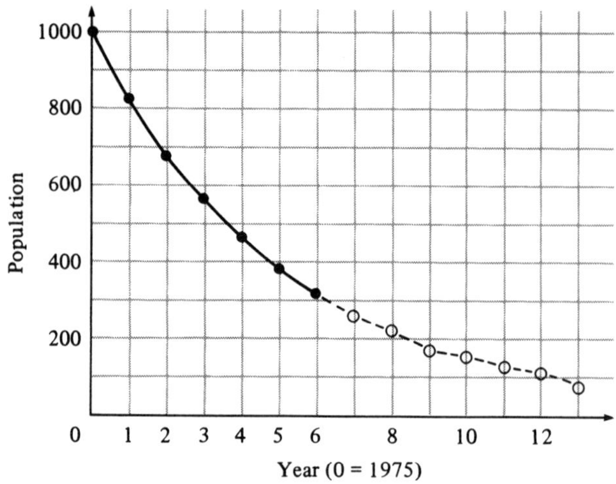

Figure G

A function will be exponential if the percentage increase or decrease is constant. For the figures given in the table for this question the annual percentage decreases are as follows.

Year	1	2	3	4	5	6
% decrease	17.0	16.9	17.4	17.5	17.0	16.7

(For example, in year 3 the actual decrease was 120 butterflies (690 – 570). The number at the beginning of the year was 690, and hence the percentage decrease was

$$\frac{120}{690} \times 100 = 17.4 \text{ (correct to 1 d.p.).}$$

As these percentages are approximately constant, the function is approximately exponential.

(b) From part (a) the decay function is approximately

$$p(t) = (0.83)^t \times 1000.$$

(If 17% are lost, then 83% remain at the end of the year.)
Thus in 1984 (year 9) the population will be approximately $(0.83)^9 = 0.187$ of the original population, i.e. approximately 190 butterflies (correct to two significant figures).
By repeated evaluation of $(0.83)^t \times 1000$ it is seen that when $t = 13$ the population is about 89. Thus the population will probably drop below 100 in year 13, i.e. in 1988.

4.3 The exponential function

12 1 (a)

x	$^-2$	$^-1$	0	1	2	3	4
2^x	$\frac{1}{4}$	$\frac{1}{2}$	1	2	4	8	16
y	$1\frac{1}{4}$	$2\frac{1}{2}$	5	10	20	40	80

(b) See Figure H.

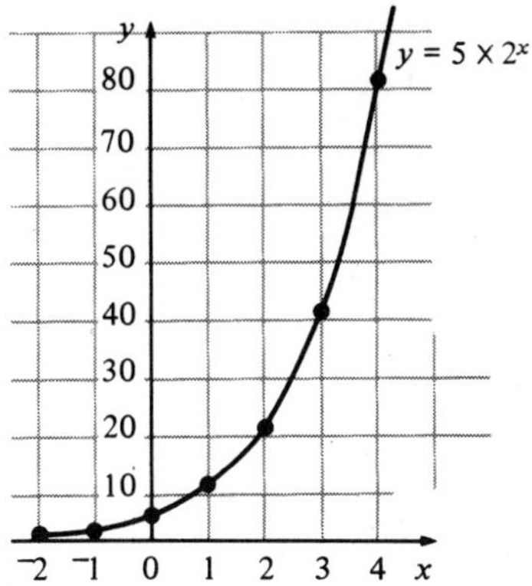

Figure H

(c) 14, 28, 56
(Unless you have drawn a very large graph you will not be able to read these results very accurately.)

13 **2** (a) The area remaining covered at the end of each month is now 98% of that covered at the beginning of the month. The decay factor is therefore 0.98. (The unit of time is still 1 month.)

(b) The formula for the area, A m^2, still covered after n months is

$$A = 36 \times (0.98)^n.$$

Hence the area still covered at the end of the year is

$$36 \times (0.98)^{12}\ \text{m}^2 = 28\ \text{m}^2 \ \text{(to 2 s.f.)}.$$

(c) Evaluating $36 \times (0.98)^n$ by repeated multiplication by 0.98 (on a calculator) gives

$$36 \times (0.98)^{35} = 17.7\ldots$$

Hence the area covered will be half the original value after 35 months. Alternatively, using the result of part (b) (28.25 correct to 4 s.f.), the formula for the area still covered after t **years** is

$$A = 36 \times (0.78)^t.$$

(The decay factor 0.78, given by $\dfrac{28.25}{36}$, is the factor when the unit of time is 1 year.)

Putting $t = 3$, the area remaining covered after 3 years is 17.4 . . . m^2, and so the area will be halved in just under 3 years.)

3 (a) With 1979 as the initial year, the initial population is 355.
14 The decay factor is constant at 0.92, and so the population function is

$$p : t \rightarrow 355 \times (0.92)^t.$$

(b) On this basis 1991 is year 12, and the estimated population for year 12 is

$$355 \times (0.92)^{12} = 130.5\ldots = 130 \ \text{(to 2 s.f.)}.$$

(c) 1971 will be year ⁻8, and so the estimate of the population in 1971 is

$$355 \div (0.92)^8 = 691.7\ldots = 690 \ \text{(to 2 s.f.)}.$$

Exercise C

15 1 (a) The decrease is 670, the number in 1977 was 2670, hence the percentage decrease $= \frac{670}{2670} \times 100 = 25.093\ldots = 25.1$ (to 3 s.f.).

(b) $\frac{500}{2000} \times 100 = 25\%$, $\frac{380}{1500} \times 100 = 25.3\%$, $\frac{280}{1120} \times 100 = 25.0\%$, and $\frac{210}{840} \times 100 = 25\%$

As these percentages are all approximately equal, the 'population' function is exponential. The decay factor is 0.75 as at the end of any year only 75% of the cars that were roadworthy at the beginning of the year are still roadworthy.

(c) The number of cars roadworthy in 1984 will be

$$630 \times (0.75)^2 = 355 \text{ (approximately).}$$

(d) By continued multiplication by 0.75, it can be seen that in 1989 the number of roadworthy cars will have fallen to 84.

(e) The original number of cars was

$$2670 \div (0.75)^7 = 20\,000 \text{ (approximately).}$$

2 (a) The formula is

$$p = 60\,000 \times (1.03)^t.$$

(b) 1984 will be year 9. Hence the estimated population for 1984 is

$$60\,000 \times (1.03)^9 = 78\,300 \text{ (to 3 s.f.).}$$

(c) Since $60\,000 \times (1.03)^{18} = 102\,146$ the population will first exceed 100 000 in year 18, i.e. in 1993.

4.4 Money

16 1

	(a)	(b)	(c)	(d)
Interest	£10.50	£123	£4.80	£222
Total amount	£110.50	£1123	£64.80	£2622

17 2 (a) £118.50 (b) £8.92½ (c) £320 (4 months = ⅓ of a year) (d) 3p

18 3 (a) When $t = 2$, $A = 500 \times (1.095)^2 = 599.51$
When $t = 3$, $A = 500 \times (1.095)^3 = 656.46$
(b) When $t = 10$, $A = 500 \times (1.095)^{10} = £1239.11$

19 4 (a) When $t = 6$, $A = 500 \times (1.0475)^6 = £660.53$
(b) To find the value of the investment after ten years, t must be given the value 20, as the interest is added half-yearly.

When $t = 20$, $A = 500 \times (1.0475)^{20} = £1264.88$

This is about £25 more than when the interest is compounded annually. In fact, to give the same total amount of £1265 after 10 years would require an interest rate of nearly $9\frac{3}{4}\%$ if the interest is compounded only annually.

Exercise D

20 **1** (a) The interest added on the 31st December 1980 is the simple interest on £500 for 4 months at a rate of 9.5% p.a.; i.e.

$$\frac{£500 \times 9.5 \times 4}{100 \times 12} = £15.83.$$

The value of the investment on the 1st January 1981 was £515.83.

(b) From the 1st January 1981 to the 30th June 1983, the growth is exponential; with initial value of £515.83, a growth rate of 1.0475, and a time interval of 5 half-years. Hence the value of the investment on the 1st July 1983 is $£515.83 \times (1.0475)^5 = £650.54$.

(c) The interest for the final two months is the simple interest on £650.54 for 2 months ($= \frac{1}{6}$ of a year) at a rate of 9.5% p.a.; which is

$$\frac{£650.54 \times 9.5 \times 1}{100 \times 6} = £10.30.$$

The final value of the investment is £650.54 + £10.30 = £660.84. (Note that this gives about 30p more than if the interest had been compounded half-yearly from the date of the investment!)

2 (a) A rate of 9.1% p.a. $= \frac{9.1}{365}$% per day = 0.0249% per day (to 4 d.p.).

(b) An original investment of £100 would be worth £100.0249 on the following day. Since £100.0249 = £100 × 1.000 249, the growth factor when the unit of time is 1 day is 1.000 249.

If the interest is compounded daily, the value of the investment after 1 year will be $£500 \times (1.000\,249)^{365} = £547.57$. This can be calculated directly if you have a $\boxed{y^x}$ button on your calculator; otherwise two alternative methods are:

(1) The logarithm of $(1.000\,249)^{365} = 365 \times \log(1.000\,249)$
$= 365 \times 0.000\,108\,13$
$= 0.039\,465\,9$

which is the logarithm of 1.095 130 7 (using the $\boxed{10^x}$ button).
In other words, $(1.000\,249)^{365} = 1.095\,130\,7$.
Hence the final value is £500 × 1.095 130 7 = £547.57.

(2) Let $1.000\,249 = a$. Calculate $n = a^3 = 1.000\,747$.
Calculate a^{365} using the relation

$$a^{365} = \frac{((((((n^2)^2)^2)^2)^2)^2)^2}{n \times (((a^2)^2)^2)^2},$$

using the $\boxed{x^2}$ button and memory.

Note that a rate of 9.1% compounded daily is as good as a rate of 9.5% p.a.

Post-test

21 **1** (a) $P = 1000 \times a^t$

(b) Putting 2000 for P and 8 for t gives $1000 \times a^8 = 2000$.

Hence $a^8 = 2$.

Using the $\boxed{\sqrt{x}}$ button

$a^4 = \sqrt{2} = 1.414\ldots$

$a^2 = \sqrt{1.414\ldots} = 1.189\ldots$

$a = \sqrt{1.189\ldots} = 1.0905\ldots$

The growth factor is 1.09, correct to 3 s.f.

(c) When $t = 50$, $P = 1000 \times (1.09)^{50} = 76\,000$ (to 2 s.f.).
(Since $a^8 = 2$, $a^{16} = 2^2 = 4$, $a^{32} = 4^2 = 16$, etc.
Hence $a^{50} = a^{32} \times a^{16} \times a^2 = 16 \times 4 \times 1.189\ldots = 76.109\ldots$)

(d) Only 1% of the population survives the non-breeding season.
Hence to provide a starting population of at least 1000 next year, the final population this year must be at least 100 000.
For this to be so, then $1000 \times (1.09)^t \geqslant 100\,000$,
or $(1.09)^t \geqslant 100$.
We know that $a^{50} = 76.109\ldots$
By repeated multiplication by 1.09 $a^{51} = 83$, $a^{52} = 90$, $a^{53} = 99$ and $a^{54} = 107$ (all to the nearest whole number).
Hence a breeding season of at least 54 days is necessary.

2 (a) The simple interest $= \dfrac{£1000 \times 12 \times 0.75}{100} = £90.00$.

(b) If the interest is compounded every 3 months, then 3% is added on at the end of every 3 months. The total amount after 9 months will be $£1000 \times (1.03)^3 =$ £1092.73, and hence the interest earned is £1092.73 – £1000 = £92.73.

(c) If the interest is compounded daily, then the rate of interest is $\frac{12}{365}$% per day, and the time is approximately 274 days.
The total amount after 9 months is therefore

$$£1000 \times (1.000\,32)^{274} = £1094.25,$$

and hence the interest earned is £94.25.

3 (a)

Year	1976	1977	1978	1979	1980
Decrease	60	55	45	40	35
% decrease	12.2	12.8	12.0	12.1	12.1

From these figures it is seen that approximately 12% of the area of 'wetlands' is lost each year; therefore at the end of any year the area of 'wetlands' remaining is about 88% of the area at the beginning of the year. Hence the decay factor is 0.88 (approximately), and the area is an exponential function of the time.

(b) If 1980 is taken as year 0, then the area of 'wetlands' in year t will be given by the formula

$$A = 255 \times (0.88)^t.$$

In 1984 (year 4), the area remaining will be $255 \times (0.88)^4 = 153$ ha (approximately).

(c) By repeated multiplication by 0.88 it can be shown that the area remaining in year 7 is 104 ha, and the area remaining at the end of year 8 is 92 ha (approximately). The area of remaining 'wetlands' will first fall below 100 ha in 1988.

(d) Working backwards from 1975 (i.e. by repeated division of 490 by 0.88), it can be shown that the area of 'wetlands' in 1970 was about 930 ha, and the area at the end of 1969 was about 1055 ha. Hence the area of 'wetlands' was last 1000 ha in 1970.